CLASSIC JAM...

CAROLINE SULLIVAN was the mistress of a large
Jamaican household at the end of the last century.
She was the author of the first ever book on the
island's cooking, *The Jamaica Cookery Book*, of
which this is a lightly revised edition.

CLASSIC JAMAICAN COOKING

Traditional Recipes and Herbal Remedies

Caroline Sullivan

Illustrations by Mary Stubberfield

Serif

London

This edition first published 1996 by
Serif
47 Strahan Road
London E3 5DA

Originally published in Kingston, in a slightly different form,
as *The Jamaica Cookery Book* by
Aston W. Gardner & Co. in 1893.

British Library Cataloguing-in-Publication Data.
A catalogue record for this book
is available from the British Library.

Library of Congress Cataloging-in-Publication Data.
A catalog record for this book
is available from the Library of Congress.

ISBN 1 897959 15 X

Designed by Ralph Barnby
Photoset in North Wales by
Derek Doyle & Associates, Mold, Clwyd
Printed and bound in Great Britain by
Biddles of Guildford

CONTENTS

FOREWORD

For many British and American people today, the Caribbean island of Jamaica evokes thoughts of paradisal holidays, days spent on white palm-shaded beaches, nights under a canopy of phosphorescent stars heavy with the smells of 'ganja weed', fresh thyme and the spiced fragrance of allspice leaves. Frying coconut oil scenting the trade winds is the essential smell of Caribbean cooking and redolent with memories for those who have spent time in the islands.

For those who would like to deepen their experience, Caroline Sullivan's collection of recipes and marvellous common sense provides an excellent foundation from which to try to capture some of the techniques and flavours of Caribbean cooking. When I first travelled to the Caribbean in 1970 Jamaica had recently become independent and I was completely beguiled by the strangeness of the produce, smells and tastes. I began to hang about in the doorways of local kitchens and was young enough to inspire sympathy in the cooks, who often felt that I looked as if I needed 'feeding up'. This way I sampled a cuisine that I could only marvel at and was hard put to imagine where its roots lay.

Moved by all this to want to write about it, I found a mass of journals and diaries from the sixteenth to the nineteenth centuries that described the dining tables of the Great Houses, but there was almost nothing published on the subject of food and its historical influences so complete and revealing as Caroline Sullivan's book. It is invaluable for all lovers of the West Indies and its unique cuisine.

Caroline Sullivan was not an innovator but a superb recorder of mid-nineteenth century Great House living in Jamaica. 'My desire,' she wrote, 'is merely to introduce to newcomers to Jamaica our own native methods of cooking our own pro-ducts ...' And although she modestly refers to her efforts as 'this little work', many of the recipes she includes could also, with a judicial change of a few ingredients, have been served at the tables of the great country houses in England.

In 1655 Cromwell seized Jamaica from the Spanish as part of his grand 'Western Design' and many English landowning families went to Jamaica, which quickly became the most productive of the sugar-producing islands in the Caribbean. The wealth made from the sugar industry supported a lifestyle of incomparable opulence. 'As rich as a West Indian planter' was a common expression in England to describe people of great means. The island was divided into great sugar-producing estates, their names – Westmorland, Windsor, Chatsworth and Cornwall – resounding with nostalgia for England. The Great Houses were built in classic proportions with elegantly carved fret-work adorning the spacious verandas and wooden jalousies decorating the great Palladian windows. They were set in vast parklands shaded by enormous spreading jacaranda trees with violet bell-like blossoms and their branches dripping with green Spanish moss and epiphytes.

It was in such a setting that Caroline Sullivan spent her life. Her family went back to the Cromwellian invasion and clearly lived in the grand colonial style. When she came to run the Great House in the mid-nineteenth century Jamaica was still enjoying and practising all the advantages and influences of England's pre-industrial taste in food and cooking. But there was a difference, for Jamaica's population was predominantly Afro-English. The English owned the great estates and organised the sugar trade, while the African (who had been transported there to plant and harvest the sugar cane) lived in small chattel houses within sight of the Great House. The result of such close proximity of two extraordinarily different cultures was a culinary marriage which is still quite unique.

Caroline Sullivan captures this for us in remarkable detail. She had a real interest in every aspect of the day-to-day running of the household, which I can hardly imagine would have met with approval in those times, since this was normally the housekeeper's responsibility. She was clearly also a remarkable observer and not above travelling to the local markets run by the African, even though tradition was that the Africans would take their produce to the back door of the Great House for inspection. This was not always an easy undertaking for, like all West Indian colonies, most of Jamaica's towns were on the coast, and during the six months of rain each year roads were frequently washed away and travel inland had to be by canoe.

Both land and sea in that part of the world provided an abundance of food. The warm tropical waters provided lobster, turtle, snapper, king-fish, shark and old wife, while the creeks, morasses, swamps and rivers provided oysters, crayfish, mountain mullet and wild fowl. Here Caroline marries traditional English Worcester and anchovy sauces with Jamaica pepper and pepper wine; lime-juice is substituted for lemon, while the classic mix of butter and parsley retains its place. Even today salt fish dishes are among those most in demand. Caroline wrote that in England salt fish was then seen as a penitential dish, while in Jamaica it was as popular among the natives as the upper classes.

Her sound common sense and wide knowledge as a working cook is in evidence throughout her book. She insisted that her readers should already have English cookery books which would guide them in the basic cooking of beef, mutton, poultry or pork. Her knowledge of the difference in pricing between town and country must have been invaluable too, and she warned her readers that newcomers might be disconcerted to find that the butcher always served equal amounts of beef and bone. This is still so today and it takes a strong stomach to watch the dismembering of a fresh carcass, flesh and splintered bone flying through the air under the not always expert chop of the cutlass. She also knew that the best saddle of mutton came from the salt ponds or from the grazing pens and was not to be fobbed off with mutton which was in fact old goat, that suet from a mountain-fed goat was better for pastry then the local beef suet, that meat could be tenderised by wrapping it tightly in a towel and burying it in a deep hole for two hours, that nothing could remove the taint of meat that had fed on guinea weed. She must have been a marvellous cook and was obviously always prepared to get into the kitchen, for she writes of successfully overcoming some of the prejudices of visitors who enjoyed her preparation of goat, unaware of what they were eating until afterwards.

In the mid-eighteenth century the majority of seeds taken from England to Jamaica failed, but by the mid-nineteenth century successful planting techniques had been established and an amazing range of fruit and vegetables was available on the island. Caroline Sullivan's knowledge of tropical tubers and the banana family is clearly the fruit of years of study and is still indispensable to any real cook of Caribbean food. She wrote that 'plantains green, plantains ripe, plantains turned' were all liked by the people and the visitor. The Africans put them in their soups and salt fish and it was *de rigueur* to serve them wrapped up in a napkin to accompany the planter's cheese. Tropical fruits abounded and from pineapples, grenadillas, guavas, ackees, mangoes and many more she imaginatively made stews, puddings, preserves, custards and jellies.

Caribbean cooking is strongly intertwined with our own historical and culinary traditions. The ingredients called for in this book are now widely available in Britain and the United States, making it possible to recreate this marvellous but little-known cuisine so evocatively described a century ago by Caroline Sullivan.

Cristine MacKie

PREFACE

I do not think I am mistaken in saying that up to the present time a book on native cookery has never been produced in Jamaica, and it is to supply this want that I place before the public the few simple receipts it has been my pleasant occupation to gather together from time to time. I am quite aware that the various methods of cooking here mentioned may be open to criticism. There are doubtless ways known superior to those a knowledge of which I have succeeded in obtaining. But faulty as they may be, I venture to hope that those here given may be of some little assistance to newcomers, on whose special behalf this work has been undertaken.

I do not venture to offer any hints to those whose long residence in the island renders them familiar with all the details of our ordinary Jamaica cooking; but from them I should be glad to receive notes on any articles which I may have omitted.

I have carefully refrained from giving European cookery, and have confined myself entirely to the everyday dishes which come under immediate notice in this island. Simple as these receipts may be, should any of them prove to be of help and use, I shall feel amply repaid for any trouble I may have taken in collecting them.

C.S.
St Andrew
Jamaica
December 1893

SOUPS

TURTLE SOUP

This is prepared in many ways, some preferring it thin, others thick. A good family soup may be made as follows.

Two pounds of turtle stew meat
Cloves
Cinnamon
Mace

Three pints of water
One large onion or some spring onions
A sprig of parsley
Some herbs
A few tomatoes
Six cloves
A piece of salt pork and a piece of salt beef
Thickening of flour
Sauce
Lime-juice
Salt
Cayenne pepper
One wineglass of sherry

Get two pounds of turtle stew meat or a little less and stew it down the day before you make your soup, with cloves, cinnamon and mace. Next day put the stew and its gravy into three pints of water with half a pound of turtle soup meat; add an onion or some spring onions (some people put a turnip and a carrot), some parsley, herbs and tomatoes. When it has boiled for half an hour, add the salt pork and salt beef cut in pieces. Let it boil for another hour, then remove any fat, dice it and put it in the tureen with some of the soft gristle as well. Let the soup boil for another half-hour, adding water if too low; then strain it through a colander. Put the strained soup back in the pot and put in a good tablespoon of flour previously mixed smooth with water; then add a little Worcester or Harvey's sauce, the juice of a lime, some salt and a little cayenne and stir till it is nice and thick like cream. Pour this over the fat and

gristle-dice in the tureen and serve, adding just
before serving a wineglass of sherry.

OKRA SOUP

Two dozen okra
Four pints of water
Indian kale or calaloo
One and a half pounds of salt beef
Seasoning
Tomato
Spring onions
Thyme
A penny-halfpenny worth of salt pork

Put the okra into the water and boil until the seeds
turn red; then add the pork and beef and go on
boiling, adding the seasoning and other ingredients.
Finely chop some kale or calaloo, add it to the soup
and serve. The soup can be strained if preferred. A
few black crabs boiled and added to the soup make
it excellent.

SUGAR BEAN SOUP

A penny-halfpenny worth of fresh green sugar beans
Three pints of water
Some bones of soup meat and a little salt pork
Black pepper
Spring onions
Herbs

Add the beans to cold water and bring to the boil. When half-done add a little soup meat and some salt pork. If preferred, the beans are left in the soup and it is then served unstrained. Children are especially fond of it, particularly if a little potato or yam is also boiled in with it. The addition of a few tomatoes is according to taste.

RED PEA SOUP

One pint of peas
Four pints of water
A penny-halfpenny worth of salt pork

Put the peas into cold water and boil for three hours or until soft, adding a penny-halfpenny worth of salt pork about two and a half hours after boiling has begun. At the end of three hours press the peas through a colander. Serve with diced dry toast.

WHITE PEA SOUP

This is prepared in the same way as red pea soup.

N.B. The natives do not strain their pea soup: they

eat the whole thing boiled with yam, coco and dumplings and often with a remarkable concoction called 'foo foo' which consists of yam or coco boiled and beaten and then added to the soup. Needless to say, this makes them a decidedly substantial repast. The dumplings are often made with equal parts of flour and cornmeal.

LOBSTER SOUP

One lobster
One pint of fish stock
Butter
Milk
Nutmeg
Pepper
Salt
Parsley
Thyme
Lime-peel
Breadcrumbs
One onion

Boil the lobster, seasoning the water it was boiled in. Put all the meat, except the tail-ends and any corals into a mortar with the shell and pound it all together as fine as possible. Add this to the fish stock and the water the lobster was boiled in; season with pepper and salt, parsley, thyme, lime-peel and some breadcrumbs and an onion. Simmer quietly for nearly two hours then strain it off. Have ready the tail-end of the lobster, diced, and the lobster corals and put them into the tureen. Add a little milk, a dessertspoon of butter and some nutmeg to the soup and give it one boil. Pour into the tureen and serve: some people like forcemeat balls added to this soup.

JONGA SOUP

This is prepared similarly to crayfish or bisque soup.

Half a dozen large jongas (freshwater crayfish)
Butter
Seasoning
Grated lime-peel
Breadcrumbs
Onion or spring onions
Milk
Butter

Half-fry the jongas in butter, then pound both flesh and shells together (but reserve one or two whole, to be cut into dice and served with the soup); pound them in a mortar, season highly, adding some grated lime-peel, breadcrumbs, onion or spring onions with the usual herbs. Add water. Boil gently for an hour, strain and put back in the pot for a little while with the diced jongas. Add a little butter (about a teaspoon) and half a cup of milk. Stir well and serve hot.

ACKEE SOUP

Take twelve ackees: pick them well, taking out the pink part. Put them into a piece of muslin and boil them. Put on two pints of water, one pound of beef and a small piece of salt pork or salt beef to make it tasty; also some seasoning, thyme and spring onions. Mash the ackees until they are quite smooth and mix them with the soup and boil them all together.

COCONUT SOUP

One pound of beef
Two pints of water
One small piece of salt pork or beef
Two small white cocos
Spring onions
Thyme
One coconut
Half a pint of hot water

Put one pound of beef with a piece of salt beef or salt pork, two small white cocos and some spring onions and thyme to boil in two pints of water. Boil down to one pint. Grate a small coconut, throw half a pint of hot water on it, then squeeze out the milk. Pour this milk into the soup and boil up, once. Before putting the coconut milk into the soup, the soup must be quite boiled and strained, then add the milk to the boiling soup. Stir well and serve at once.

PEPPER POT

Three tablespoons of pure casseripe to every
two pints of cold water
Salt to taste
A handful of bird peppers or cayenne pepper
Meat
Eggs

Get an earthenware vessel. To every two pints of cold water, add three tablespoons of the pure casseripe with salt to taste and a handful of bird peppers. If these cannot be had, use some cayenne. Cut the meat into small pieces after being well cooked, and put into the pot: boil well for half an hour. Any sort of meat may be used, and hard-boiled eggs are an improvement. It should be warmed every day, and something added each day.

PUMPKIN SOUP

One large slice of pumpkin or half a small pumpkin
Three pints of water
Some soup meat or a little salt pork or salt beef
Black pepper
Thyme
Curry-powder

Cut up the pumpkin, add it to the water putting with it the soup meat (if fresh meat) and a little thyme and black pepper. Bring to the boil. In about half an hour add a small bit of salt pork or salt beef, or else salt to taste. In about another half-hour strain the soup through a colander and serve curried: this soup is particularly palatable.

FISH

Snappers, mullet, king-fish, mackerel, old wife, calepeaver, cutlass, mountain mullet, lobsters, crayfish, oysters, jongas, crabs, shrimps and turtle all have their season in Jamaica.

There are two sorts of crabs, the white and the black. The former are not generally eaten, being foul feeders, but the black crabs are highly esteemed and are counted among the delicacies of Jamaica.

KING-FISH

This is a much esteemed fish, and is good cooked in any way. Boiled and served with butter and parsley or oyster or anchovy sauce, it must be appreciated by everyone. King-fish steaks, that is, king-fish cut up into thick slices and broiled with onions, are excellent, especially if a rich brown gravy is added. Opened and stuffed with breadcrumbs and oysters and served with tomato sauce, they make a rich and agreeable dish.

MOUNTAIN MULLET

These are esteemed one of Jamaica's delicacies. They are of excellent flavour but the drawback to them in many people's opinion is the number of small bones they possess. The nicest way of cooking them is rolling them in buttered paper and frying them, sending them to table in the paper, but they can of course be fried plain or boiled if preferred.

CUTLASS

This is a long ribbony fish and it has small bones at the side, which must be carefully taken away; very good cutlets can be made of this fish, but it also makes excellent fish cakes or fish pies. They do well for kedgeree, a mixture of boiled rice, picked fish, mustard, butter and curry-powder.

CALEPEAVER

This fish is sometimes called the salmon of Jamaica. It is a very rich, delicately flavoured fish, most often to be had in the vicinity of Spanish Town. The size varies, but they are sometimes very fine and large. The best way of cooking this fish is to boil it; putting it on (after carefully cleansing it and rubbing it with lime-juice) in hot water with a little salt in it, boiling slowly, allowing ten minutes' boiling to each pound of fish. Shrimp and butter sauce or oyster sauce are good additions, but perhaps butter and parsley is best, and a cut lime handed round for its juice to be squeezed over the fish.

JONGAS

Jongas are a kind of small crayfish which are often found in the mountain rivers. They are cooked like lobsters and make an excellent stew, fricasee or curry.

OYSTERS

Of these there are two sorts, the round or raw-eaten oyster and the flat or cooking oyster. The former are small but very delicate in flavour; they can of course also be cooked. The flat oyster is the best for scallops or patties, or in any cooked form. The way to open them is by placing them near the fire so that the shells open of themselves.

ROAST LOBSTER

More than half-boil a lobster, then take it out of the water and shell it as quickly as possible. While hot, rub it well with butter, put in a Dutch oven, baste it well until nicely frothed and serve with melted butter.

LOBSTER CROQUETTES

One small lobster
Seasoning
Tomato
Spices
One onion
Lime-juice and lime-peel
Butter
Cream or milk
Grated bread
Two eggs

Shell a small lobster and chop it fine with seasoning and nutmeg, onion, tomato, pepper and thyme, with a little grated lime-peel and some of the juice of the lime and some salt. Add a dessertspoon of butter and about as much cream or milk and two tablespoons of grated bread. Mix all together with two beaten eggs: make balls, roll in egg and breadcrumb and fry. Put either a rich white sauce or brown gravy in the dish, the croquettes on the top, and serve very hot.

BAKED LOBSTER

One lobster
One tablespoon of butter
Plenty of pepper and salt
Worcester sauce
Jamaica pepper or pepper wine
Vinegar
Breadcrumbs
Butter

Boil the lobster, then shell, pick and chop it fine. Add a tablespoon of butter, plenty of pepper and salt, a little Worcester sauce and some Jamaica pepper just to flavour, or some pepper wine; a little vinegar too. Mix all these ingredients well together, put them in a small buttered pie-dish, breadcrumb it, put a little dab or so of butter here and there and bake.

LOBSTER CUTLETS

Half a pound of lobster flesh
Two ounces of butter
Two teaspoons of chopped onions
One teaspoon of flour
Water
Milk
Salt
Pepper
Cayenne
Parsley
Two egg yolks

Cut up the lobster. Put two ounces of butter and two teaspoons of chopped onions in a saucepan; add the lobster and fry for a minute or two. Stir in one teaspoon of flour mixed smooth with water; add half a pint of milk, salt, pepper and cayenne; two teaspoons of chopped parsley. Let it boil a little, stirring all the time: add the lobster, give it a boil, add the two egg yolks; mix quickly and put into a dish to cool. When cool and firm, divide into six parts and shape like cutlets; egg and breadcrumb twice. Put a piece of the very small claw to the end of each cutlet so as to form a bone; fry for a few minutes, as you would a sole, in plenty of lard or fat; lay on a cloth and serve on a napkin with plenty of parsley. No sauce is needed. The lobster may be prepared, shaped and breadcrumbed some hours before wanted.

OLD WIFE

These are queer flat fish. They should be cooked like the English sole. Wash them carefully and dry them well, then dust over a little flour; egg and breadcrumb them, and fry a light brown, turning them when one side is done. Serve with melted butter and garnish with parsley.

JUNE FISH

A cottony fish. It should be stewed in a rich brown sauce with onions, tomatoes and herbs, with a glass of port added towards the end of the cooking and thickened with a little flour. A little fresh pepper makes an agreeable addition, but very little.

BAKED FISH NO. 1

Clean, rinse and wipe dry any kind of fish; rub with salt and pepper; fill with stuffing, the same as for poultry, only drier. Sew up and put in a pan with some hot dripping and a lump of butter. Dredge with flour and lay over the fish a few thin slices of salt pork or dab with bits of butter. Bake for an hour and a half, basting occasionally.

BAKED FISH NO.2

Any cold fish
Macaroni
Milk
Grated cheese
Breadcrumbs
Cayenne

Boil in milk twice as much macaroni as you have cold fish until it is soft. The cold fish should be broken into small pieces and the bones removed. Mix the fish with the macaroni, which should be cut in dice, the grated cheese and cayenne. Put it in a flat dish with breadcrumbs and some pieces of butter on the top and bake a light brown. Any fish will do for this dish.

TURTLE CUTLETS

One and a half pounds of turtle steak
Onions
Pepper
Lime-juice
Salt
Bread or biscuit crumbs
Nutmeg
Tomato
Spring onions
Two eggs

Cut the turtle into cutlets, rub well with onion and sprinkle with pepper, sauce and lime-juice. Get ready some bread or biscuit crumbs; add nutmeg and some onion or finely minced spring onions and tomatoes. Dip the cutlets into the eggs previously stirred in a plate, then into the seasoned crumbs. Cover well and fry, serving with cut lime and parsley.

TURTLE BALLS

One and a half pounds of turtle
A small piece of salt beef
Seasoning
Tomato
Spring onions
Lime-juice
Herbs
Two eggs
One tablespoon of sherry

Mince the beef and turtle together very fine. Add some chopped tomatoes, spring onions, herbs, salt and a very little Jamaica fresh pepper; add a squeeze of lime-juice, a little sauce, a tablespoon of sherry, a little spice and two well-beaten eggs. Make into balls and fry, sending them to table with a rich, well-seasoned brown gravy, to which add another teaspoon of sherry and lime-juice.

TURTLE STEAK

Two pounds of turtle steak meat
Lime-juice
Lard
Pepper
Onions
Tomatoes
Flour
Butter

Rub the steak well with lime-juice. Have ready some boiling lard in a frying pan. Put in the meat whole. (Some people cut it in pieces, but it is really best done whole, or it is likely to get tough or dry.) Put with it some black pepper and sliced onions and tomatoes. Cover it over a little; when half-done it will make its own gravy, but if not quite enough, add a tablespoon of water and, if a thick gravy is wanted, a little flour and butter rubbed smooth together with the water. The steak takes from twenty minutes to half an hour to cook.

Serve with the fat put on the top of the meat, squeeze some lime-juice over the whole and garnish with cut lime and slices of onion and tomatoes.

TURTLE STEW

Two pounds of turtle stew meat
Two pints of water
Seasoning

Lime-juice
Cinnamon
Nutmeg
Ten cloves
One onion
A few tomatoes
Parsley
Thyme
Sherry

Take two pounds of turtle stew meat, wash it well with salt and lime-juice and put it into two pints of cold water; then add a stick of cinnamon, a large onion, a few tomatoes, some parsley, thyme, herbs and pepper.

Stew gently for three hours, adding water now and then if it gets too low. About a quarter of an hour before serving, mix a good tablespoon of flour smoothly with a little water, sufficiently liquid to pour into the pot to thicken the stew. Stir. At the last minute put in a dessertspoon of sauce and half a glass of sherry; mix well and serve with a cut lime to squeeze over the meat.

BOILED BLACK CRABS

These are liked either plain boiled or 'baked in the back' as the expression is. Plain boiled, they come to table whole and they have really more flavour that way, but there are many small bones and there is much difficulty in eating them at table. The claws contain the principal meat; the back is to be opened and the gall removed; the black water inside possesses much flavour. When in full season the eggs are numerous and excellent; boiled in soup they are delicious.

BAKED BLACK CRABS

Carefully pick the meat from all the claws and smaller bones of a dozen boiled crabs; this takes a long time and careful picking. Then open the backs and extract the eggs, throwing away the galls and putting aside the black water which is to be added again at the last minute. When all the picking is done, add two tablespoons of butter, a teaspoon of black pepper, a dessertspoon of sauce or pepper vinegar, a little cayenne and some nutmeg to the meat. Mix well, adding salt to taste, and fill as many of the backs as you can, leaving room for a dressing of breadcrumbs on which dabs of butter are placed to moisten. Before putting the meat into the backs, put one or two eggs in each shell and do not forget to mix in the black water, as that has the full black crab flavour. The twelve crabs ought to make ten good crab back fillings.

LAND TURTLE OR TERRAPIN

Cut off the head and open the back. Remove the flesh from the inside and take away the bones and also get what meat you can from the legs. Scald it with boiling water to remove the outer skin. Chop the meat into dice, adding a small piece of salt pork and salt beef, some tomatoes, spring onions, herbs and black pepper with some cinnamon and nutmeg; add some sauce, butter, lime-juice and a glass of sherry; mix together all these ingredients and put them into the turtle back. Breadcrumb the top, put dabs of butter here and there and bake in the shell. As there is not much meat in these turtles it will take two turtles to fill one back.

See Publisher's Note on p. 184.

SALT FISH

It is surprising to most newcomers to find that in Jamaica there is hardly a more popular dish among the natives, and often among the upper classes, than the despised salt fish, eaten at home not from choice but as a sort of penitential dish. Here it is the almost daily, and certainly the favourite, food of the people generally, and cooked as they cook it cannot fail to please the most fastidious.

SALT FISH AND ACKEES

One pound of salt fish
The fruit of twelve ackee pods
Lard
Butter
Black pepper

Soak the salt fish overnight. Put it on to boil in cold water, otherwise it hardens: throw off the first water and put it on again to boil. Carefully pick the ackees free from all red inside, which is dangerous, and boil them for about twenty minutes; add them to the salt fish which is then cut in small pieces; add some lard, butter and pepper. Some prefer the salt fish and ackees mashed together and the melted lard and butter poured over the top.

SALT FISH AND RICE

This is a favourite native dish. The salt fish and rice, about half a pound of salt fish to a pint of rice, are boiled together with the usual bit of salt pork and a little butter.

SALT FISH FRITTERS NO.1

Some people add an egg or perhaps two to salt fish and rice and make fritters of it for breakfast.

SALT FISH FRITTERS NO.2

Boiled salt fish and ackees mixed together with pepper and seasoning make excellent fritters. No egg is required.

SALT FISH FRITTERS NO.3

Half a pound of salt fish
Jamaica pepper
Tomatoes
Spring onions
Butter
Lard
Parsley
Two eggs

Boil half a pound of the fish and mash it fine with some seasoning, a tablespoon of butter, a teaspoon of lard, a little chopped fresh Jamaica pepper (or some cayenne) and some minced tomatoes, spring onions and herbs. Mix well with two well beaten eggs and fry in fritters. These are very good for breakfast.

SALT HERRINGS

Soak the herrings well. Then boil them, changing the water once or they may be too salty. Drain and serve with melted butter and parsley and garnished with slices of fresh pepper, fried onions and tomatoes.

SALT MACKEREL

Soak the fish for some hours, then boil it, changing the water once to extract the salt. Put it on in cold water and let it come to the boil. Drain and serve with butter sauce, garnished with sliced limes, tomatoes and fresh peppers.

FRIED SALT FISH

Half a pound of salt fish
Onions
Tomatoes
Lard
Butter
Pepper

First boil the fish. Then cut it into medium-sized pieces and fry with slices of onions and tomatoes, which should be served on the top of the fish with slices of pepper and some parsley.

SALT MACKEREL CUTLETS

Soak the mackerel for some hours; boil it, putting it on in cold water. Then cut the fish into slices, egg and breadcrumb and fry with lard.

SALT FISH TWICE-LAID

Half a pound of salt fish
Four large potatoes or a good slice of any yam,
except the yampee which is too sweet
One tablespoon of butter
One dessertspoon of lard
Parsley
Pepper
Spring onions
Tomatoes
Herbs

Boil the fish, chop and mix it well with the mashed potato or yam, add the butter and lard, herbs and other ingredients. Mix in two beaten eggs; butter a pie-dish, put in the mixture and bake a light brown.

CURRIED SALT FISH

Salt fish stewed in the way mentioned in these recipes and then curried, with the addition of a spoonful of mustard, is a very acceptable dish. Put a tablespoon of curry-powder and a squeeze of lime-juice to the mixture and serve with rice balls.

SALT FISH AND SUSUMBERS

Boil the salt fish after soaking it for a few hours; while it is boiling add some of the young susumber berries to the fish and boil till tender. They give it a bitterish taste highly appreciated by the natives, but not palatable to everybody, and one must be careful to choose the right kind of susumber as there are two varieties. This dish is served with melted butter and lard poured over it.

SHREDDED SALT FISH

Soak some salt fish for two hours, pull it to pieces in shreds and fry with lard, adding spring onions, tomatoes and pepper.

SALT FISH PATTIES

Half a pound of stewed salt fish
Spring onions
Tomatoes
Pepper
Onion
Butter
Sauce
Parsley and herbs

Half a pound of salt fish stewed with some spring onions, tomatoes, pepper and a dessertspoon of butter. Add a little sauce and nutmeg. Put in patty-pans lined with pastry. Cover and bake.

NOTE

The 'salt fish' referred to in this chapter is most usually salt cod, although fish such as coley and saithe are sometimes used. This can be bought in Jamaican and other Caribbean shops and also in Italian, Spanish and Portuguese delicatessens, but is best had from the former which sell the darker flesh favoured in Caribbean cooking rather than the white flesh used in European salt cod dishes. The salted and dried fish should be soaked in fresh water for 24 hours, stirring and changing the water at least twice to remove the salt.

MEAT

Beef, mutton, pork and poultry are to be had in markets all over the island, and in the country parts distant from a market there are always butchers who supply pork, or goat mutton at 6d per pound. Now and then a cow is killed in the district and then notice is given.

In this little work I do not allude to any methods of dressing beef, sheep mutton, pork or poultry, for my desire is merely to introduce to newcomers to Jamaica our own native methods of cooking our own products, and by no means to attempt to cope with the many excellent works that at present exist on English or other cookery. It will be noticed, therefore, that nothing will be mentioned here except a few hints that may be of service to those who are strangers to our native dishes, provided as they must already be with cookery books which will guide them in the cooking of beef, mutton, pork or poultry.

There will be some surprise and perhaps discomfort on the part of the newcomer who finds that beef of all cuts is sold at the same price, 6d per pound, no matter what one orders, unless one arranges with the butcher to give beef without bone at 7½d per pound; this of course would only be practical with a round steak or a fillet. But the butchers charge 6d per pound for bone as well as meat, and sometimes one is disappointed to find that when the 'meat' is delivered, one half of it is 'weigh meat' or large pieces of bone. Sheep mutton is sold at 1s per pound, sometimes 10½d. Pork from 6d to 7½d, oftener 7½d; in the country parts it is always 6d, the liver at 4½d, head 4½d per pound. Poultry ought not to fetch more than 9d per pound in the towns, 6d in the country parts, or at the highest 7½d per pound. In and about Kingston the people hawk them about asking exorbitant prices; it is always best to weigh them. Ducks vary from 10½d to 1s per pound; turkeys 1s per pound; pigeons 1s 6d a pair for the large, 1s 3d for the smaller. Wild birds vary in price, from the small ground dove at 3d each to the larger birds going from 1s, 1s 6d, 2s to 2s 6d and 3s a pair. Guinea birds 2s 6d each or 3s. Wild guinea birds 2s 6d each or 5s to 6s per pair.

KID OR GOAT MUTTON

It is undeniable that a good deal of the so-called 'mutton' offered for sale in Jamaica is nothing else than goat, either old or young. Not that real mutton cannot be had, and when one does get it, one gets something good; nothing can be better than a saddle of mutton from Salt Ponds or the mutton from the grazing pens throughout the island. Nevertheless a hint or two may make a goat dinner palatable instead of 'sending the hungry empty away'. In the first place prejudice goes a great way. I have heard people say over and over again that no matter how disguised 'goat mutton' may be, they would never eat it. Yet these very people have enjoyed it in my presence, so much so in fact as to ask for another helping. But I confess that on the other hand, if one has to depend on a cook who is no real cook at all and can only 'roast and boil' (as she thinks, which is again another matter), one may find a tough, stringy, inedible mass served up with a quantity of grease and water as gravy, enough to make paterfamilias enraged and the housekeeper in no enviable frame of mind.

I do not say that all or any of the recipes I give here will necessarily meet with the approval of all those who try them; but where one may be dissatisfied another may be pleased, and all my endeavour is to make the best of an inferior thing when one cannot get the best.

WET GRILL OF KID OR GOAT MUTTON

Thin slices of cold, roast or boiled mutton
One tablespoon of flour
One tablespoon of butter
Three tablespoons of mustard
Pepper
Salt
Nutmeg
Worcester, John Bull or Harvey's sauce
Cayenne

Take some thin slices of cold mutton. Put them on a large plate and score lightly on both sides. Press some pepper, butter, sauce, mustard, nutmeg and a little salt into the scores. Do this on both sides. Make a sauce as follows. Rub up in a basin a tablespoon of flour with a tablespoon of butter, three teaspoons of made mustard, a little cayenne pepper, a little nutmeg, a teaspoon of salt and a dessertspoon of Worcester, John Bull or Harvey's sauce. Worcester is best. Rub all these together as smooth as you can, adding by degrees a teacup of water. Throw this sauce into a frying pan and set over the fire, or it can easily be done over a small nursery stove. Stir until it is well mixed and begins to thicken, then put in the slices of seasoned mutton and turn occasionally; in about a quarter of an hour it will be fit to send to table. A little roast or burnt sugar added to the sauce gives it a nice colour. Should the sauce be too thick, a little more water can be added.

STEWED KID OR GOAT MUTTON

Meat
Beans or peas
Thyme
Pepper
Water
Tomatoes
Flour
Cloves
Parsley
Herbs
Spring onions
Lime-juice

Put on the mutton in enough cold water to cover it, adding five cloves. Let it stew gently for about an hour, then add a little pepper, spring onions, tomatoes, some parsley and herbs. If you want sugar beans or broad beans served with it, put these in now; the mutton is excellent, done with either of those beans or with cockle cress peas or even with very young goongoo peas (the green ones). Turnip and carrot can, of course, be used instead. When the vegetables are tender, add a little salt, a little lime-juice and a thickening of flour to the gravy. The stew will take about two hours; do not let the water dry in the pot or the meat will burn.

KID OR GOAT MUTTON CUTLETS

Thin slices of mutton
Sauce or vinegar
Pepper
Salt
Nutmeg
Two eggs
Breadcrumbs
Lard
Sliced lime

Pour over some thin slices of cold mutton, a little mushroom or other sauce, or some vinegar; sprinkle with salt and pepper and a little nutmeg, egg and breadcrumbs and fry with lard. Serve with thin slices of lime on each cutlet.

Note. For a large tough joint, wrap it tightly in a towel. Dig a deep hole and bury it for two hours. Then take it out and roast. It will be very tender and the flavour will be immensely improved.

MUTTON WITH GUINEA-HEN WEED

Avoid this altogether. The people soak the meat in vinegar, which they fondly hope destroys the detestable taste of the weed, but it cannot do so completely and once smelt or tasted it cannot be mistaken. Sometimes beef tastes and smells of it too. Avoid that also.

KID MUTTON SUET

Sometimes a mountain-fed goat will have really a surprising amount of suet. This makes almost better pastry than beef suet.

MUTTON KIDNEYS

Grilled or stewed in the usual way, and served on toast buttered and peppered.

BOILED KID OR GOAT MUTTON

Meat
Water
Salt

Put the joint on in boiling water, adding a little salt when about half-done. This meat can be sent to table with carrots or turnips as garnish, or boiled with sugar beans or with onion sauce to which a little milk and flour has been added.

CURRY OF KID OR GOAT MUTTON

The remains of a joint or the chops can be curried, making a sauce of water, flour, butter, mustard, curry-powder, a little lime-juice and very little coconut milk. Serve with rice balls.

ROAST KID

I have seen a small kid roasted and stuffed like a roasting pig. If in good order, it is a dish by no means to be despised, but it is ugly in appearance. A leg of kid, weighing about four pounds or less, is generally rubbed over with butter and put into a dutch oven. This is occasionally basted, and when served up a little flour is added to the gravy to thicken slightly.

KID OR GOAT MUTTON PIE

The remains of roasted or boiled goat or kid mutton
Pepper and salt to taste
Tomatoes
Spring onions
Parsley
Nutmeg

Potatoes
Eggs
Flour
Butter
Sauce
Bacon or ham
Pastry

or

The remains of some boiled or roasted cold kid or
goat mutton
Pepper and salt to taste
Some chopped tomatoes
Parsley
Spring onions

Cut the mutton in nice pieces. Line a pie-dish with pastry and put either bacon or ham on the bottom and sides. Next, put some of the hard-boiled eggs (cut in thin rounds) here and there. Then bits of ready-boiled potatoes or small bits of yam. Make about a pint of rich gravy with the mutton bones, a little flour to thicken it and some sauce; add the chopped spring onions, tomatoes, pepper and salt to taste. Arrange the meat in the pie-dish, filling up the spaces with bits of egg, yam or potato, and ham or bacon; pepper all well. Pour in the gravy (the best sauce to use is mushroom); if not quite full, add a little flour mixed with a little salt and water. Cover with pastry and bake.

GOAT OR KID MUTTON TIMBALE

*The remains of a joint of kid or goat mutton that has
been either roasted or boiled
Macaroni
Three tablespoons of grated cheese
Two large or six small tomatoes
One onion
Black pepper
Salt
Parsley
Thyme
Two eggs
One tablespoon of butter
Ham or salt pork
Nutmeg
Milk*

Remove any tough outer skin or gristle from the joint and dice it. Add to this some macaroni, about an equal quantity of mutton and three tablespoons of grated cheese. Take two large or six small tomatoes, one onion, some black pepper, parsley and thyme. Chop all these fine and mix with the above. Beat two eggs well and add them to the mutton and other ingredients, adding a little milk; put in a tablespoon of butter, about a tablespoon of minced ham or salt pork, a pinch of nutmeg and some salt. Mix all thoroughly together and put in a buttered mould. Boil for an hour and a half and serve with a good brown gravy.

VEGETABLES

PLANTAINS

Plantains green, plantains ripe, plantains turned. All are appreciated by the West Indian and are popular with our visitors. Green, they are eaten boiled or roasted. The people put the green plantains and also the green bananas in their soups, or eat them with their salt fish. Green roasted plantains are *de rigueur* with the planter's cheese, served up in a folded napkin. Boiled they are eaten too as vegetable, but not when very ripe, and they are less palatable that way. 'Turned' is when they are between green and ripe, and they go excellently well with salt fish or eaten boiled or roasted with butter put inside them. Ripe, they are very good indeed roasted and particularly good when cut in thin slices and fried or cut in pieces with butter inside. A breakfast dish is made of either green plantains or turned plantains roasted, then chopped in dice, or fried if preferred, and sent to table with melted butter poured over them.

PLANTAIN TARTS

Take very ripe plantains, boil them and let them cool. Then mash them very smooth. Sweeten to taste, adding spice also to taste. Then colour the mixture a deep red with the juice of the prickly pear. Put on thin pastry; fold and bake.

PUMPKIN AND RICE

One large piece of pumpkin
Half a pint of rice
Spring onions
Tomato
Butter
A penny-halfpenny worth of salt pork
A dessertspoon of butter

A good-sized piece of pumpkin is boiled with rice and mixed well with a little chopped spring onion and tomato, a little pepper, a dessertspoon of butter and a penny-halfpenny worth of salt pork, cut in dice. This is a favourite dish among the natives.

PUMPKIN FRITTERS

Half a small pumpkin
Butter
Pepper
One egg
Lard

Half a small pumpkin boiled until tender and then mashed well with a little butter, black pepper and one egg. When well mixed, put it in spoonfuls in a large saucepan and fry, turning till cooked each side.

Omitting the pepper and substituting sugar to taste, these make delicious sweet pumpkin fritters.

BOILED PUMPKIN

This can be served in two ways. The natives prefer it boiled and cut in 'junks' with a shake of black pepper over it. The more refined way is to mash it with some butter, salt and pepper and shape it in the dish.

PUMPKIN PIE

One round pumpkin
One pound of minced meat
Spring onions
Seasoning
Salt
Pepper
Butter

One round pumpkin, one that can stand in a dish, not one that rolls over. Cut off the top, about a third of the vegetable. Then scoop out all the seeds and pithy stuff round them. Cut out the pulp as close to the rind as possible, just leaving enough near the rind to keep it from breaking. Boil this pulp; meanwhile have one pound of meat minced and seasoned with pepper, salt, butter and spring onions. Pack this into the hollowed-out pumpkin rind, put on the cover, that is the top that has been cut off (with the stem on if possible), and bake for three-quarters of an hour. Serve with the top on and with a folded napkin round the lower part.

BOILED MOUNTAIN CABBAGE

Procure a large bit of the mountain cabbage: peel and boil it, serving it with thick white sauce.

Mountain cabbage is extremely nice even eaten raw, but it is then decidedly indigestible.

INDIAN KALE

One large bunch of Indian kale
A penny-halfpenny worth of butter
Pepper
Milk
Salt

Boil a large bunch of the kale and chop very fine like spinach, with butter, a little salt and black pepper; if milk is to be had, a tablespoonful is a great improvement.

ARROWROOT

Arrowroot is bought here at 6d for two pints and Jamaica arrowroot is generally preferred, being very white and light. English cookery books give so many excellent ways of preparing it that it is unnecessary for me to say much about it here.

TOUS-LES-MOIS

This is sometimes called French arrowroot. It is made from a bulb which can be eaten as a vegetable boiled like yam or coco but it is generally made into flour. It is supposed to bear every month, hence the name. It is far better to buy it ready made at 6d or 7½d a pound than to make it at home; the process is tiresome and takes up time. It must be first grated into water, then well washed and dried, then sifted.

It is more nourishing than arrowroot but is prepared precisely in the same way as pap, thin or thick as liked, and it makes an excellent pudding prepared according to any ordinary arrowroot recipe.

ACKRA CAKES

Two pints of black-eye peas
Cold water
Fresh country pepper and a little cayenne
Lard

Take two pints of black-eye peas and soak them in water overnight; in the morning the outer husk will be easily rubbed off. Then pound the peas finely on a large smooth stone and mix in a fair amount of fresh country pepper and a little cayenne. Then beat up the mixture in a large basin with a wooden spoon until it is very light. Have ready plenty of boiling lard or oil, then drop in the mixture in spoonfuls and in a few minutes the ackras will be cooked. They must be a light brown.

BOILED WILD CUCUMBERS

Take the very young ones and throw them into salt and water for a short while. Then boil them till tender. They can then be served with melted butter and a sprinkling of pepper. The nicest way, however, is to smother them in white sauce.

YAMS

These are various. There are the white yam, the guinea yam, the hard yam, the yellow or affoo yam, the negro yam, the Lucea yam and the Indian yam. The white yam is excellent roasted or boiled and mashed with butter; it is sometimes called 'flour yam' from its floury nature; the skin when roasted is delicious. The yellow yams vary, some being waxy, others floury; they are eaten boiled or roasted but the skin is bitterish, though some people like it. Sometimes it is grated and sent to table (after boiling).

These hints apply also to all the other yams. Some of them are white, others of a dark purple and very delicate in flavour. The Indian yam, or yampee, is somewhat sweet.

YAM BALLS

One large slice of yellow, white or negro yam
Butter
Salt
Pepper
Two eggs
Lard

Boil a large slice of yam. Mash it well with some butter; put some black pepper and salt to it and two beaten eggs. Form into balls and fry in lard.

YAM STUFFING

A large slice of yam
Salt
One tablespoon of butter
Spring onions
Tomatoes
Herbs
One egg

A large slice of yellow, negro or white yam. Boil and mash it with a tablespoon of butter, some chopped spring onions and tomatoes, herbs and a beaten egg. Add some salt. This makes very good stuffing for roasting pig.

YAM PIE

Minced yam
Spring onions
Tomatoes
Onion
Salt
Butter
Herbs
One egg

Mince some meat of any kind and season well with tomatoes, onion, spring onions and herbs, a little salt, butter and sauce. Put this at the bottom of a well-buttered pie-dish. Boil and mash a good piece of yam (except the Indian yam), mix with it a little butter and salt and one beaten egg. Spread over the mince and bake.

SLICED YAM

Peel and slice pieces of yam very thin: fry them in lard and send hot to table, or put the slices on a gridiron, buttered, turning the slices till both sides are cooked.

SWEET POTATOES

These are liked by many visitors to Jamaica and form a substantial assistance to the food of the people. They are as a rule very cheap. They are eaten like yams, boiled, roasted or cut in thin slices and fried. The natives also make an excellent pudding of them which goes by the name of sweet potato pone (see p.74).

COCOS

Cocos can be boiled or roasted. They are harder than yams. The roasted coco skin is very nice eaten with butter. The grated coco is also very good; it makes good fritters and boiled coco mashed with butter is another way of serving it.

COCO FRITTERS

Grate one large raw coco. Add a beaten egg, a little salt and butter and a teaspoon of flour. Moisten with milk and fry in lard.

ARRACACHA

This is a kind of yam and has a peculiar flavour rather like parsnips; it is not common. It is cooked in the same way as yams are.

ACKEES

Ackees are a delicate tree vegetable and, if carefully prepared for table, are most enjoyable, but if eaten before the fruit opens on the tree, or if forced ripe, musty or over-ripe, a more unsafe edible could not be found. They are excellent boiled, fried or curried, and they make a rich soup.

I have myself made a nice pudding, substituting ackees for eggs; it was much appreciated. I put as much of the vegetables as would hold in about six of the pods, stirring them in after mashing fine with the ingredients to make an ordinary bread pudding.

Salt fish is often mixed with ackees, and forms one of the popular Jamaican luncheon or breakfast dishes, as do salt fish fritters made either with seasoning and eggs or with ackees instead of eggs. See pages 37–43.

FRIED AUBERGINE

Cut some small aubergines in thin slices with the skin on. Fry in lard, crisp.

STUFFED AUBERGINE

One large aubergine
Mince
Butter
Pepper
Herbs

Take a large aubergine and cut it open the long way. Take out the inside, leaving the backs to form a sort of dish. Boil the pulp until tender and mix with it some well-seasoned mince and a little butter. Put it into the scooped cut backs, breadcrumb over it and put some dabs of butter on the top and bake.

DRIED OKRA

Cut some okra slices in the short way and put them

on a sheet of paper in the sun to dry. Turn them now and then, and in about three days they will be dry enough. These can be put in a parcel and sent to England or elsewhere to be made into soup: they will keep good some time, especially if sunned occasionally.

CASSAVA FLOUR (QUACHO)

Grate the sweet cassava root and wash it as for starch. Dry well in the sun, pound it in a mortar and sieve it. Squeeze all the water well out and then dry it.

BAMMYS NO.1

Bammys are sold ready for cooking and are a sort of muffin. They are made out of cassava, but they do not keep long so are better eaten fresh. They are to be put on the gridiron till done, turning them till both sides are brown, then split open and buttered.

To make these cakes, the bitter cassava is grated, pressed and then put into iron hoop moulds. The bammy cakes are very thick; the cassavas thin, less of the butter being put at the bottom of the moulds.

BAMMYS NO.2

Grate sweet cassava root, and squeeze it (without

washing) in a cloth, a little at a time. Bake it between stones or in a pan until firm. When wanted to be eaten, soak the cake in milk, toast it, cut it in half and butter it.

PURSLEY OR PURSLANE

Young shoots of pursley
Butter
Salt
Pepper

Choose the young shoots and boil them. The natives eat it with their salt fish, or chopped and put in okra soup, or chopped fine and mashed like spinach, and mixed with butter and salt and sprinkled with black pepper.

TAPIOCA NO.1

Take the sweet cassava root and grate it. Put it in a cloth and pour water on it, rubbing in the water well with the hand, letting it run through a cloth into a pan or yabba, below. Allow this to settle; pour off the water; now take a clean yabba and put in a little of the starch at a time to bake. When done put it in the sun to dry well, then pound it in a clean mortar and it will be fit for use. Should you make it of the bitter cassava, you must wash the starch twice. The refuse of the sweet cassava can be used to make cakes.

TAPIOCA NO.2

Grate some cassava and prepare as for starch. Pass it through a sieve when not quite dried and place it on a tin sheet over the fire. Keep it moving, in case it burns.

CHO-CHO

The cho-cho is a very useful vegetable; it can be cooked in various ways and the natives are very partial to it, it being, as they say, 'so cooling'. They often put it in their soups as an addition. Plain boiled with butter or white sauce, it is excellent; mashed with butter and black pepper, it is nice. Put in stews, it makes a pleasant variety, and made into boiled puddings with a judicious addition of sugar and lime-juice, it so much resembles apple as to deceive one into believing one is eating apple pudding or apple tart. The baked pudding is particularly good.

STUFFED CHO-CHO

Two cho-chos
Butter
Black pepper
Salt
Mince
Seasoning
Breadcrumbs

Boil two cho-chos with the skin on. When boiled scoop out the insides (cutting the cho-chos the long way). Remove the seeds and pith; pare away the pulp carefully, leaving enough near the rind not to break through it. Mash the pulp with some nicely seasoned fine mince, to which add a little butter and pepper and pack the mixture into the cho-cho backs or skins. Cover with fine breadcrumbs and bake. A nice side dish.

Puddings and
Preserves

STEWED PINEAPPLE NO.1

One black pineapple
Two pounds of sugar
Cinnamon
Water

Cut off the skin of a full, but not ripe, black pineapple, or one of the common sort; a Ripley does not do so well. Take out any little black seeds. Slice the pineapple into about half-inch slices, removing the hard middle. Put the slices in a saucepan with about two pounds of sugar and enough water to cover them. Stew with a little cinnamon until the syrup thickens, then set it aside to cool.

STEWED PINEAPPLE NO.2

One pineapple
Water
Half a pound of sugar to each pound of fruit

Peel the pineapple and grate it. Put the pulp into a saucepan with a little water and half a pound of sugar to each pound of pulp. While this is boiling put on another pan with the skins and heart in enough water to cover them and boil that too. Then strain and add to the pulp with an extra half-pound of sugar. Boil a little while. Bottle while hot and cork down tightly.

PINEAPPLE JAM

One common pineapple
Spice
One pound of white sugar
One pint of water

Peel and remove the seeds and hard centre of a common pineapple. Chop fine, season with spice and put it in a stewpan with one pound of white sugar and about a pint of water. Stew till it gets to the consistency of jam. This can be eaten hot served with rice round it and warm milk of coconut cream; it also makes excellent tartlets with pastry or it can be eaten cold as jam with bread and butter.

STEWED GRENADILLA

Open the fruit and remove the seeds, strings, etc. Peel it and put the outer pulp into a saucepan, after cutting it into large pieces (about the size of a walnut) with very little water, a half cupful or so. Add cinnamon and one pound of sugar, and stew till the sugar becomes syrup. This is nice for tarts. A finer sort can be made by cutting the grenadilla finer before stewing; this makes good tartlets.

GRENADILLA FRITTERS

The outer pulp of a grenadilla
Two tablespoons of sugar
A little spice
Two eggs
Lard
Sifted sugar

After having taken out the inner pulp, juice and

seeds, skin the fruit and mash the outer pulp fine. Mix this with two tablespoons of sugar, but before this pour off any unnecessary water. Then add spice and two well-beaten eggs. Fry in a pan with some boiling lard, turning till done on both sides. Serve with sifted sugar over them.

ORANGE AND COCONUT OR ANGELS' FOOD

Peel some oranges and remove all the white skin. Divide them into segments, removing all the skin also from each segment, leaving only the inside pulp. Put this in a glass dish and grate coconut thickly over it. This makes a very pretty and enjoyable dish.

GUAVA PUDDING

Two eggs
Their weight in flour and butter
One cup of stewed guava or of guava jelly
A pinch of soda
Two tablespoons of sugar

Beat well together and steam for two hours.

STEWED GUAVA

Two dozen ripe guavas
Water
Cinnamon
Cloves
One pound of sugar

Peel and core two dozen ripe guavas and throw each as done into a basin of water. When all are ready, put them in a saucepan with enough water to cover them, then put in some cinnamon and cloves and one pound of sugar. Tie all the seeds in a muslin bag and put this also with the fruit. Stew all together till the fruit is tender and then set aside to cool, removing, of course, the muslin bag and its contents.

Eaten cold with milk, custard or coconut cream, or even without any of these, it is delicious.

YAM PUDDING

One slice of yam
One tablespoon of butter
Spice
Rosewater
Sugar
Two eggs

Mash a large slice of boiled white yam with a tablespoon of butter, some spice, rosewater and sugar to taste. Beat up two eggs and, if liked, add a little milk; mix all together and bake in a buttered pie-dish.

SWEET POTATO PONE

One large sweet potato
One tablespoon of yam or coco
One beaten egg
One tablespoon of butter
Half a grated coconut
Milk
Black pepper
Water
Two tablespoons of sugar

To one large boiled and grated sweet potato put a tablespoon of grated yam or coco, one beaten egg, half a grated coconut made into coconut milk, or else a little cow's or condensed milk, nutmeg, black pepper (plenty) and two tablespoons of brown sugar in half a cup of water. Put in a 'pudding pan', as they call the little round baking tins, and bake until firm.

ORANGE CUSTARDS NO. 1

The juice of a sweet orange and half the rind
One spoonful of brandy
Four ounces of loaf sugar
Four egg yolks
One pint of cream or milk
Preserved orange

Boil till tender half the rind of a sweet seville orange. Beat it fine in a mortar, put on it a spoonful of brandy, the juice of the orange, four ounces of loaf sugar and the yolks of four eggs. Pour in a pint of boiling cream or rich milk by degrees and keep beating until cold. Then fill up the cups and place them in an earthenware dish of hot water till set. Stick preserved orange on the top and serve either hot or cold. Iced is best.

ORANGE CUSTARDS NO.2

Slice oranges. Pour over them a custard with half a pint of milk and the yolk of one egg. Sweeten to taste. Pour this cold over the sliced oranges, on the top of which put the white of the egg beaten to a thick froth with a little sugar.

BUTTERED ORANGE-JUICE

The juice of three seville oranges
Four teaspoons of rosewater
The yolks of six and the whites of four eggs
Half a pound of powdered white sugar
A dessertspoon of butter

Mix the juice of three seville oranges with four teaspoons of rosewater. Add the well beaten yolks of six and the whites of four eggs and half a pound of powdered white sugar. Stir over a gentle fire till it is thick, putting in a lump of butter a few minutes before it is taken off the fire. Stir this well through the mixture, then pour into a glass dish and serve cold.

BANANAS FOR DESSERT

Slice bananas and pour cream and sugar over them.

FRIED BANANAS

Cut the fruit in three, lengthways: dip each piece in flour and fry in hot butter. Drain on paper and serve very hot. Hand sugar and lemon with them.

FRUIT SALAD NO.1

Sliced pineapple
Sliced banana
Sliced oranges

Strew sugar over all and serve in a glass dish.

FRUIT SALAD NO.2

One pineapple
One mango
One naseberry
One orange
One banana
Two slices of musk-melon
Two slices of water-melon
One tablespoon of curaçao or mareschino
Half a grated coconut
One tablespoon of brandy

Cut the pineapple in half. Squeeze out and set aside the juice of the first half. Peel the second half and cut in dice, removing the hard part. Put this in a large glass dish. Take the mango, peel it and cut away the cheeks, throwing away the skin and stone. Cut the cheeks in dice and add to the pineapple. Skin and stone the naseberry and add that in pieces to the other fruits. Peel the orange and remove all outer and inner white skins; add this also (if any orange-juice escapes, add it to the pineapple-juice). Peel and cut the banana in small bits and put that in too. Peel and seed the melon slices, cut the flesh in dice and put that in as well, and do the same with the water-melon. Mix them all lightly together and pile up high. Add a tablespoon of either curaçao or mareschino and a tablespoon of brandy to the juice of the pineapple and the orange. Pour this over the fruits in the glass dish; over the top of all put lightly half a coconut which has been previously peeled and grated. Ice well.

TAPIOCA PUDDING

Half a cup of tapioca soaked overnight
One pint of cold water
Half a cup of sugar
Half a cup of jam
Two egg whites

Half a cup of tapioca soaked overnight in a pint of cold water until soft. Then mix with half a cup of white sugar and half a cup of jam. Boil, stirring all the time until clear. Mix with two beaten egg whites and then pour into a wet mould. Ice when cold.

ACKEE PUDDING

Ten ackees
Nutmeg
One pint of milk
Cloves
Sugar
One egg

Boil the milk with some sugar, nutmeg and cloves. Mash the ackees fine. Beat an egg, add the milk and mix in the ackees. Pour the mixture into a buttered pie-dish, grate some nutmeg over it and bake.

PUMPKIN TART

Stew the pumpkin in a little water and rub through a sieve. To twelve tablespoons of pumpkin, add two ounces of butter, six eggs, a little ground cinnamon, the juice and part of the rind of a lime, a cupful of milk, sugar to taste and two spoonfuls of ginger. If the mixture be too thick, thin with warm milk. Add half a glass of wine or brandy – or both mixed. Make a thin paste, put in the prepared pumpkin and bake.

PUMPKIN PUDDING

One large piece of pumpkin
One tablespoon of butter
Sugar to taste
Half a cup of milk
Spice
Rosewater
One egg

Boil a good-sized piece of pumpkin, taking out all the seeds, etc. Mash it well with a tablespoon of butter, half a cup of milk, sugar to taste, some spice, rosewater and one well-beaten egg. This can be eaten baked either with a crust or not, but the crust improves it.

GUAVA JELLY

Four dozen guavas
Two pints of water
One pound of sugar to every two pints of juice

This is very troublesome to make and must be carefully done. Take four dozen guavas and put them on to boil, whole, in a large pot with two pints of water and let it steam down, covered, for two hours, making its own juice; take it off the fire and put it all into a sieve, which must be placed over a large basin or some receptacle to catch the draining, for it must drain all night. Next day measure the juice and for every two pints put one pound of sugar and boil the sugar and juice with spices. Skim the mixture as the scum rises until it is perfectly clear, and when very thick pour it off to harden and cool.

COCONUT PUDDING NO.1

One sponge cake
One teacup of milk
Two ounces of coconut
One egg
Pounded sugar

Butter a small dish; cut a sponge cake in slices and place in the dish. Mix the yolk of an egg with a teacup of milk and pour it over the cake; then strew two ounces of grated coconut over it. Next beat the white of an egg to a froth, add a little powdered sugar and beat together with it. Put over the top and bake in a moderate oven. A dutch oven will do this dish nicely.

COCONUT PUDDING NO.2

Four ounces of butter
Eight ounces of powdered sugar
Four ounces of grated coconut
Two ounces of shredded lemon
One grated lime-rind
Four eggs
Lime-juice

Mix together the butter and the powdered sugar and place them over a slow fire. When this has boiled for two minutes pour it out to cool. Mix it with four ounces of grated coconut, two ounces of lemon, shredded small, one grated lime-rind and four well-beaten eggs. Mix all well together and then add the lime-juice. Pour into a buttered pie-dish and bake a nice brown. This pudding is decidedly improved by having a crust.

GRATED COCONUT

Grated coconut is served with curry and is much appreciated.

GISADAS

One grated coconut
Brown sugar to taste
Nutmeg
Cinnamon
Rosewater
One egg
Pastry
Coconut water

Grate the coconut. Then add brown sugar to taste, with the coconut water, a little nutmeg, cinnamon, rosewater and one beaten egg. Have ready some patty-tins lined with pastry, put in the mixture, pinch the sides and bake. These are open tartlets.

BOILED CHO-CHO PUDDING NO.1

Four ounces of grated bread
Four ounces of currants
Three tablespoons of sugar
One lime
Two large cho-chos

Mix the bread, currants and sugar together; add the cho-chos (mixed as described below) and then the well-beaten eggs. Pour into a buttered mould with a cover and boil two hours.

To prepare the cho-chos for pudding

Boil two large cho-chos with eight cloves and a small bit of cinnamon till tender. Remove the seeds and strings, after which mash the cho-chos well and squeeze out all the water, which will be plentiful. This will be easily done by putting them into a clean dry cloth and wringing them well. Mix this pulp with a couple of tablespoons of sugar, some grated nutmeg and the squeezed juice of a lime. It is impossible from the varying sizes of the cho-chos to be perfectly accurate as to the exact proportions of the sugar and lime, but either can be added until you are satisfied with an apple-like taste. Often more of both sugar and lime will be required. The pudding can be eaten hot with sugar sauce, or cold with a custard round it.

BOILED CHO-CHO PUDDING NO.2

Three cho-chos
One egg
One tablespoon of corn starch
One tumbler of milk
Sugar to taste
Lemon or vanilla essence

Prepare the cho-chos as before and put them at the bottom of a glass dish. Make a custard with the yolk of one egg, a tablespoon of corn starch and a tumbler of milk sweetened with about four tablespoons of sugar and flavoured with either lime-peel, essence of lemon or vanilla. If lime-peel, soak it in the milk for a quarter of an hour previous to use. Boil the mixture, stirring till thick; when cool, pour over the cho-chos. Beat the white of the egg to a stiff froth with a tablespoon of crushed sugar and put on the top. Eat very cold; it is best iced.

CHO-CHO AND GROUND RICE PUDDING

Four good-sized cho-chos
Lime-juice
Sugar
Cloves
Spice
Milk
Water
Ground rice
One egg

Boil four good-sized cho-chos and prepare as for boiled cho-cho pudding. Take a dessertspoon of ground rice and boil it with a pint of milk and water. Sweeten when half-done, add cinnamon and spice. Beat up one egg well and add to this till it thickens. Put the cho-cho into a pie-dish and the custard over it. Grate some nutmeg over the top and bake.

Excellent hot or cold.

Tous-les-mois may be substituted for ground rice if preferred; make it the same way.

BAKED CHO-CHO PUDDING

Four good-sized cho-chos
Ten cloves
Two limes
Half a pound of sugar
Half a pint of milk
One tablespoon of butter
Nutmeg
Breadcrumbs
Three eggs

Four good-sized cho-chos boiled with ten cloves and mashed and prepared as before, only putting the juice of two limes, half a pound of sugar, one tablespoon of butter and some nutmeg. Put the mixture at the bottom of a well-buttered pie-dish and cover it with a pint of grated bread. Beat the yolks of three eggs and one egg white and add to them half a pint of milk sweetened to taste; pour this over the breadcrumbs and bake. When it has 'taken colour' and is nicely baked remove it from the fire. Then beat the other two egg whites into a stiff froth and add the two tablespoons of sugar; when stiff spread over the pudding. Put back in the oven for a couple of minutes to colour a pale yellow. It is nice either hot or cold.

CHO-CHO TART

Six good-sized cho-chos
Three quarters of a pound of sugar
Twelve cloves
One grated lime
The juice of two limes
Pie crust

Line the pie-dish with pastry and leave some to cover the tart. Take the six cho-chos; pare, core and boil them with a dozen cloves. When tender slice them not too thin and put at the bottom of the pie; sprinkle them with the sugar, the grated lime-peel and the lime-juice, then cover with pastry and bake for half to three-quarters of an hour. Eaten when cold with a cold boiled custard it is much appreciated, but it can be served hot like apple tart.

COCONUT, TOUS-LES-MOIS AND GUAVA PUDDING

One egg
One dessertspoon of tous-les-mois
One pint of water
One grated coconut
Stewed guava
Nutmeg

Make a custard of one egg, one dessertspoon of tous-les-mois and one pint of water into which a coconut has been grated, squeezed and strained. Butter the pie-dish. Put in a layer of stewed guava with some syrup. Pour the custard over, grate some nutmeg on the top and bake.

STEWED WATER-MELON

Pith of water-melon
Rosewater
Water
Half a pound of white sugar
Cinnamon

There is a good deal of pith near the rind of the water-melon which is generally not made much use of. It can however make a nice preserve. Cut it in small pieces removing the rind. Put it in a stewpan with very little water and rather more than half a pound of white sugar, a stick of cinnamon and a tablespoon of rosewater. Let the sugar boil to a syrup, turning now and then in case it sticks, and then turn out to cool. Cut in very much larger slices, it can be similarly stewed and made into a tart with pastry.

BREADFRUIT PUDDING

One ripe breadfruit
Nutmeg
Cinnamon
Rosewater
One tablespoon of butter
Half a pound of sugar
One tablespoon of sherry or brandy
Two eggs

Ripe breadfruit is to be chosen for this; after having peeled it, mash it into pulp with a fork. Then add plenty of nutmeg, cinnamon and rosewater, a tablespoon of butter, about half a pound of sugar, a tablespoon of sherry or brandy and two well-beaten eggs.

Eaten with a crust this is excellent. Some people make it yet richer by the addition of raisins, currants and candied peel.

ROAST BANANAS

Six or eight bananas
Sugar
Lime-juice

Put the bananas in their skins into the ashes and roast them for about half an hour. They will then look black. Serve them up just as they are in their skins. At table run your fork right down the side and lay them open. Dust some sugar over the fruit inside, adding a squeeze of lime-juice and eat with a spoon and fork.

BANANA FRITTERS

Half a dozen ripe bananas
One tablespoon of milk
Two eggs
Spice
Flour
Lard

Half a dozen ripe bananas peeled and mashed fine. Mix with them a tablespoon of milk (this can be omitted if preferred) and two beaten eggs; add some spice and enough flour to form a stiff paste. Put in a frying pan heated with lard and fry. Serve with sifted sugar over them and a slice of lime on each fritter.

BAKED BANANAS

Slice some bananas lengthways and put in a well-buttered pie-dish. Sprinkle sugar and lime-juice over them and bake.

BOILED BANANA PUDDING NO. 1

One cup of dried bananas
One cup of breadcrumbs
Three-quarters of a cup of sugar
One cup of suet (or two ounces of butter)
One teaspoon of mixed spice
Two eggs
Lime-juice
Candied peel

One cup of dried bananas chopped fine; a squeeze of lime-juice; (a little candied peel is an improvement), mix the dry ingredients and then add the two well-beaten eggs. Butter a mould and boil the pudding for three hours.

BOILED BANANA PUDDING NO. 2

Six ounces of shredded bread
Two eggs
Four ripe bananas
One pint of milk
Six ounces of sugar

The juice of one lime
Cinnamon
Nutmeg
Rosewater

Mash the bananas after stripping off the skin or, if preferred, chop them in dice and add to the shredded bread with the sugar, spices, rosewater and lime-juice. Beat the eggs, add the milk and mix with the other ingredients. Put all into a buttered mould and steam for two hours.

BAKED BANANA PUDDING

Four ounces of breadcrumbs
Four bananas
Two eggs
One pint of milk
Four tablespoons of sugar
Nutmeg
Rosewater

Peel and mash the bananas and add to them two tablespoons of sugar and a squeeze of lime-juice (some like plenty); add some nutmeg and rosewater. Put this preparation at the bottom of a very well-buttered pie-dish, then put the breadcrumbs over that. Make a custard with two beaten eggs, a pint of milk and two tablespoons of sugar; pour over the whole and bake till a nice brown.

BANANA PRESERVE

Bananas can be mashed to a pulp and a little sugar and nutmeg added. Spread on the top of a cake, and between the layers in place of preserve.

IMITATION STRAWBERRIES AND CREAM

Four bananas
Strawberry jam
Milk
Egg white

Peel four bananas and remove any strings. Mash them into pulp and mix with them some strawberry jam and milk. Mix well. Serve in a glass dish, with white of egg beaten with a little sugar to a stiff froth and dropped lightly on the top just before going to table.

DRIED BANANAS

Choose good ripe bananas. Peel them and put them in the sun on perforated zinc or wire frames so as to avoid sweating. Turn the bananas two or three times during the day and continue the process for five or six days until the bananas are brown and of a mellow consistency without becoming hard. They can then be packed in tins or boxes which have been lined with paper. It is desirable to have the fruit covered with thin muslin or net while drying, on account of the flies.

PRESERVED BANANAS

Six bananas
Half a pint of water
Half a pound of sugar

Boil the sugar and water together to make a syrup. While boiling, peel the six bananas and break them into halves. Put these halves into syrup and boil till tender and the syrup is about the consistency of honey. Serve cold.

PRESERVED LEMONS

Pare and slice them the long way. Remove the seeds. Weigh the fruit. One pound of sugar to one pound of fruit. Water to cover. Boil till tender without stirring very much.

CORNMEAL PUDDING

One cup of cornmeal
Half a cup of plain white flour
Water
Milk
Butter

Two eggs
Spice
Rosewater
Four tablespoons of sugar

Mix together one cup of cornmeal and half a cup of plain white flour. Rub together, then mix with enough water to make it liquid. Boil this in a saucepan till thick and smooth. Add to it a little butter, spices and rosewater and take it off the fire; sweeten it to taste with four tablespoons of sugar, or more if liked very sweet. Beat two eggs lightly, add them to the mixture and place this in a buttered pie-dish and bake.

STEWED CASHEWS

One dozen cashews
Salt and water
Fresh water
Sugar
Cinnamon
Spice

One dozen cashews. (They stain dreadfully leaving a brown stain which cannot be removed, so care must be taken not to let drops fall on clothing, and to wash the hands after preparing the fruit for stewing.) Take the cashews in your hands, removing the seeds, and squeeze out the juice as much as possible till they look quite crumpled up. Fling them into a basin, or yabba, which has salt and water in it. This is to extract the stainy taste. Leave them there for an hour, then put them in a saucepan with water to cover them, add one pound of sugar to each pound of fruit and some cinnamon and spices. Boil until they are tender and the sauce is thick. The juice when boiled ought to be about the consistency of treacle.

MANGO TART

Pastry ·
Stewed mangoes

Line a pie-dish with pastry and fill with stewed mangoes done according to the following recipe. Cover with pastry and bake. Open tartlets can be made in the same way, but the mango for these must be chopped rather fine.

STEWED MANGOES

Green mangoes
Sugar
Spices
Water

Peel some green mangoes and cut them in bits. Throw the skins and stones away. Put the fruit into a saucepan with sugar and spices (one and a half pounds to one pound of fruit) and enough water to cover them. Stew gently till tender, adding water if it gets too low, and until the syrup thickens.

MANGO FOOL

Two large cups of ready-stewed mangoes
Milk
Nutmeg

Take two large cupfuls of ready-stewed mangoes; chop very fine indeed and then pass it through a sieve. Moisten with milk as you press it through until it is of the same consistency as gooseberry fool. Put it in custard cups, with nutmeg grated over each.

MANGO JELLY

Green mangoes
Cloves
Water
Cinnamon
Sugar

Take green mangoes when just full. Slice them, cover them with water, putting in a few cloves and some cinnamon; boil till quite soft then strain, and to each cup of juice add a cup of sugar; boil till reduced by half.

STEWED TREE-TOMATOES NO.1

Ripe tree-tomatoes
Sugar
Water

Take the ripe tomatoes and scald them with boiling water; this will allow the skin to be pared off. Then weigh the fruit, and to one pound of fruit allow half a pound of sugar. Make a syrup with a gill of water to half a pound of sugar. Some of the seeds of the tomato should be scooped out. Put the fruit into the syrup which has previously boiled up and allow it to boil until it is tender and the syrup is thick.

STEWED TREE-TOMATOES NO.2

Scald the fruit and remove the outer skin. Put the fruit into an enamelled saucepan with just enough water to cover them. Add sugar to taste and stew gently for fifteen or twenty minutes. Serve up when cold.

STEWED GREEN TAMARINDS

Tamarinds
Salt and water
One and a half pounds of light brown or
albion sugar
Cinnamon

Extract the seeds and throw the fruit into strong salt and water for a night. Throw that water away in the morning and put the tamarinds on to boil for a little while. Throw away also that second water. Then put them on with enough water to cover them and add one and a half pounds of light brown or albion sugar and some cinnamon. Stew gently, stirring occasionally till the syrup is very thick, and then turn out to cool.

RICEY COCO

Half a pint of rice
Coconut milk
Nutmeg
Cinnamon
Sugar
Rosewater

Boil a pint of rice very soft and add to it while hot some coconut milk, nutmeg, cinnamon, rosewater and sugar to taste. The people often eat this for their breakfast.

COCONUT PUDDING

One grated coconut
Four eggs
Half a pound of white sugar
One tablespoon of rosewater

Beat the eggs and sugar together till very light, add the grated coconut and the rosewater, mix well and bake with a crust.

COCONUT CREAM

One grated coconut
Two pints of water

Grate a coconut. Pour two pints of boiling water on it and skin when cold. Some people merely put the grated coconut in a coarse cloth and wring out the juice. It is a great addition to tarts, entrées or savouries.

COCONUT CUSTARDS

One pound of grated coconut
One pint of new milk
Six ounces of sugar
Six eggs

To one pound of grated coconut allow one pint of new milk and six ounces of sugar. Beat well the yolks of six eggs and stir them in the milk with the coconut and sugar. Put the mixture into a pail, pan or pitcher, set it into boiling water and stir all the time till very smooth and thick. As soon as it comes to a hard boil take it off and put it in cups or glasses.

COCONUT BLANCMANGE

One ounce of gelatine
Two pints of milk
Six ounces of sugar
Coconut
Essence of vanilla

Soak one ounce of gelatine in a pint of milk. Then put it in a saucepan with six ounces of sugar and stir till it boils; take it off and let it cool. Grate the coconut (or half a large one), add it to the water of the nut if there is any and stir into it a pint of fresh milk seasoned with a little essence of vanilla. Add this to the boiled milk and gelatine, stir well for a few minutes and then pour it into a wetted mould. It is excellent when iced.

COCONUT AND TAPIOCA PUDDING

One cup of tapioca soaked overnight
A quarter of a pint of milk
Butter
Four egg yolks
Two egg whites
One cup of sugar
Two tablespoons of grated coconut

Mix the tapioca previously soaked overnight with the grated coconut. Beat the eggs, add the milk and sugar and bake for half an hour in a buttered pie-dish. To make this richer a little butter may be added. Frost it when baked with the egg whites and three tablespoons of sugar; set it back in the dutch oven to turn a light brown and serve either hot or cold.

PRESERVED TAMARINDS

Tamarinds
Sugar

Put layers of tamarinds and then layers of brown sugar into a keg and so on until it is nearly full. Then have a large quantity of new sugar boiled down to syrup and pour it boiling on the layers. It will be fit to eat in two weeks.

TREE-TOMATOES DOLCE

Ripe fruit
Equal weight of sugar
Very little water

Take ripe fruit. Cut them across and scoop out the pulp and seeds until only a thin rind of outside is left. Then steam this with very little water. When the whole is soft rub through a sieve and allow a weight of sugar equal to the pulp. Put this into the preserving pan and keep stirring frequently as it is very apt to catch. Three-quarters of an hour to one hour is about the time the pulp will take to be boiled to a proper consistency. A brisk fire is the best.

ROSE-APPLE PRESERVE

Two dozen rose-apples
Water
Cinnamon
One pound of sugar

Peel two dozen rose-apples. Halve them, remove the seeds and little bits of stringy pithy inner skin. Put them on a very little water with some cinnamon and about one pound of sugar. Stew till tender, which will not take very long. They can be stewed either cut in half or in finger slices.

PRESERVED CAPE GOOSEBERRIES

One pint of Cape gooseberries
Salt and water
Fresh water
One and a half pounds of sugar to one pint of fruit
Cinnamon

These make a delicious preserve, but take a quantity of sugar as they are exceedingly acid. The seeds must be first extracted with a penknife, making a small hole; then the gooseberries are thrown into salt and water overnight. Throw off that water and scald them; throw that second water away too. Then put them into a stewpan with enough water to cover them; if there is plenty of fruit add more sugar, but in the proportion of one and a half pounds of sugar to one pint of gooseberries. Make a thick syrup, boiled down with a stick of cinnamon, until the fruit is tender.

PRESERVED GINGER

Ginger
Water
Sugar
The white of an egg

The months of July and August are the best for preserving ginger, as after that it is apt to be old and tough. Take only tender pieces of ginger, wash them well and put on to parboil for a little while. Being young they will not require much boiling. Take out when tender, put the pieces of ginger into cold water and scrape the outer skin off and put into fresh cold water. Change the water frequently, as it draws the heat from the ginger. Boil a thin syrup (half a pound of white sugar to one pint of water) and pour on hot to the ginger. Let it stay in that syrup for a day, then make another syrup somewhat thicker than the first, pour that on hot to the ginger which has been taken out of the first syrup. Let that remain on for a day, and then prepare the last syrup which must be thick, say one pint of sugar to a gill of water. Pour that on cold. Put the ginger in jars or bottles before putting on the last syrup. All the syrup should be clarified with the white of an egg.

TOMATO PRESERVE

Ripe tomatoes
Sugar
Water
Spices
Lime-juice

The tomatoes must be quite ripe. Pour boiling water over them to remove the skins. Afterwards, put the fruit without the skins into a muslin bag and strain the juice (throw that away). Add sugar – about half a pound of sugar to each pound of fruit – and some water; let them boil slowly till the syrup thickens. A little lime-juice, cloves and cinnamon added make a great improvement.

OTAHEITE APPLE STEW

Cut the fruit into halves and scoop out the seeds. Put in a pan with water to cover them and with half their weight in sugar. Stew till tender, adding a little spice.

MAMMEE PRESERVE

Peel the fruit and remove the seeds. Take half their weight in sugar and enough water to cover them. Boil.

Some people slice the fruit and some grate it.

SEVILLE ORANGE PUDDING

One unripe grenadilla
The rind of two seville oranges
The juice of one lime
Four eggs
White sugar
One spoonful of butter
Pastry

Grate an unripe grenadilla and the rind of two
seville oranges and mix them with the lime-juice.
Whip four eggs, yolks and whites separately.
Sweeten with pounded sugar, put in the yolks and
stir the ingredients over the fire one way, till it
begins to thicken and as it thickens stir in a spoonful
of butter and then pour into a pie-dish lined with
pastry. Mix in the whipped whites at the last before
putting in the dish. Bake for half an hour.

ICES

COCONUT ICE-CREAM

Four grated coconuts
Sugar to taste
One pint of milk

Grate the four coconuts and put them into a large
coarse cloth. Squeeze out all the juice; do not add

any water. This, properly done, ought to make a pint of cream. Mix with this one pint of cow's milk and sweeten to taste. Then freeze. It must be rather sweet as freezing makes it require a little extra sweetness.

PINEAPPLE ICE

One peeled pineapple
Lime-juice
Eight tablespoons of sugar
Water

One pineapple peeled and sliced and the hard centre removed; chop fine and bruise the pulp in a mortar, adding a little lime-juice, not quite a pint of water and eight tablespoons of sugar. Mash all together, pounding well, and then strain and freeze.

SOURSOP ICE-CREAM

Two soursops
Sugar to taste
Water

Put all the pulp but not the seeds or rind into a large bowl. Pour in two pints of boiling water; mash the pulp well in the water and strain and put to cool. When cold, add sugar to taste and half a pint of milk. Freeze.

ORANGE ICE

Six oranges
One pint of water to eight tablespoons of sugar

Peel six oranges and squeeze out the juice; some like a little of the grated peel too. Mix well, strain and freeze.

COCONUT WATER ICE

Take very young coconuts and choose those that have plenty of soft jelly. Cut up this jelly in small bits. Pour off as much coconut water as will make two pints. Sweeten this to taste, add the cut up coconut jelly and freeze.

LIME ICE

Two pints of water
Eight squeezed limes
Sugar to taste

Mix well and freeze.

BANANA ICE-CREAM

Two bananas
Three eggs
One and a half pints of milk
Sugar

Make a custard of the eggs, milk and sugar to taste. When cold, add the two bananas mashed fine and smooth. Stir, mix thoroughly and freeze.

FRUIT

SHADDOCK

Cut the skin a third of the way from the top, removing the top without cutting the inside of the fruit. This forms the cover. Now cut the skin carefully down in wedges not quite to the bottom. Take out the fruit whole, away from the skin and rind. Now take away all the thin white skin remaining on the fruit till it looks as clean as an orange. The outer peel cut in wedges is now carefully ornamented on each side by little notches each side of the wedge. The fruit is then replaced in the skin, the cover put on it and it is ready for table. Serve with two forks as it must on no account be cut with a knife.

FORBIDDEN FRUIT

This is somewhat larger than a grapefruit. It is called 'forbidden fruit' because of three brownish marks on the outside peel supposed to be Eve's fingermarks as she plucked the fruit. It is of the orange-shaddock tribe – very juicy. It is opened for table in a similar way to the shaddock and two forks are used to tear open the fruit from the centre.

GRAPEFRUIT

Is of the same tribe and is opened similarly for the table to the shaddock and forbidden fruit.

BLACKBERRIES

These grow in the hills and can of course be prepared in accordance with recipes given in English books. The country people bring them down for sale in the summer season.

GRAPES

Both the white and black grape do well in Jamaica. They are to be purchased from 1s to 1s 5d or 2s per pound.

FIGS

White and black figs grow well in Jamaica. They are generally sold by the plateful, at 6d or 9d a plate.

AVOCADO PEARS

These are chiefly eaten at breakfast or luncheon with pepper and salt. They can however be eaten as a dessert prepared at table by mashing (after removing the skin and seed) in the plate, adding sugar, nutmeg and a taste of sherry all mixed together.

BREADFRUIT

Various opinions are expressed about this fruit, some people liking it extremely and others not liking it at all. The natives are very fond of it. It can be eaten roasted, boiled or cut in slices and done on a gridiron. Roasted, it is put in the ashes about two hours before serving, then scraped and sent up whole. At table it is cut in wedges, the heart removed and it is eaten with or without butter.

Boiled, the skin is removed. The people often put it in their soups. Sliced, it is cut very thin, toasted on the gridiron, then buttered and eaten hot.

BREADFRUIT FLOUR

The green breadfruit is cut in slices and dried; then it is pounded and sifted. After this the people boil it up into a pap which they sweeten, and it forms one of their favourite breakfasts.

BANANAS

This fruit is accepted as being both nourishing and digestible. It can be cooked in various ways, besides being an agreeable and much sought after edible in its raw state. It can be used either green or ripe. The natives eat it boiled in its green state, added to their salt fish, meat or soups, and it makes many a dainty preparation in the form of puddings. The green banana sliced, dried and pounded in the mortar makes a flour which serves to make a very substantial pap, which the people find nutritious and satisfying.

SWEET CUPS

Are abundant in some parts of the country. There is a variety of them. Some are called the Pomme d'Or, others Grenadita, and so on. The outside is very hard and contains within the shell a mass of seeds and pulp much after the style of the grenadilla.

ROSE-APPLES

Many persons thinks these insipid; others praise the delicate flavour and perfume. They can be eaten raw or made into preserve. The seeds are poisonous.

ORANGES

Oranges are plentiful and easily obtained. All the recipes for orange marmalade, stewed oranges, etc, are well known in English cookery, so no mention is made of them here. Elsewhere in this book oranges and coconut, and oranges and star-apples are mentioned as being used together. There are three varieties of orange in the island; the sweet, the seville and the seville-sweet. The seville is used chiefly for floor cleaning and other purposes; the seville-sweet can be eaten raw like the ordinary sweet orange, but is better for making marmalade; or baked and eaten with sugar, hot, for a bad cold.

STAR-APPLE

Cut not quite half-way through and twist the top round; then pull and the core will come away easily and the star be plainly seen. Take the seeds away and eat the pulp with a spoon as near the rind as is agreeable. It is very sticky and gummy, but the fruit itself compensates for that.

ORANGES AND STAR-APPLES

Open the star-apples, removing the core and seeds. Put the pulp in a tumbler, squeeze the juice of the oranges onto this and add a little sugar and nutmeg and a dash of sherry; mix together well. This is called 'strawberries and cream'.

SAPADILLAS

This is a very large kind of naseberry; it is eaten with a spoon extracting the seeds; it is very luscious.

GRENADILLA

Open and take out all the seeds and pulps and the juice. Put it all into a tumbler together with some sugar, some nutmeg and a dash of sherry. Eat, seeds and all, after mixing well.

CHERRYMOYER

This fruit is eaten with a spoon, removing the seeds and not going too close to the rind. It will not require any sugar.

SWEETSOP

This is of the same tribe as the cherrymoyer; it is eaten in the same way, removing the seeds first.

PAWPAW

This is not always a favourite fruit, though some people say it is nicer than a musk-melon. It is extremely sweet, but the seeds taste like black pepper. It is cut and eaten like musk-melon only without the addition of sugar, pepper and salt.

The leaves of the tree have a peculiar quality of rendering tough meat tender. For instance, say you have a tough beef-steak (very probably you will have) or a tough fowl. Either rub them with the leaves or roll them up in the leaves for a short time. When cooked perhaps the flesh of the fowl will fall away from the bone when carving, or the steak be almost too tender. In this case the meat ought to be eaten the same day, for it is very likely to turn bad by the next morning.

CUSTARD APPLES

This a richer kind of fruit than the cherrymoyer and others of the same tribe. It has been called 'Jamaican ice-cream'. It needs no sugar and is eaten with a teaspoon, removing the seeds. It derives its name from its rich creamy flavour; it is most delicate.

GUINEPS

These stain terribly and the stain cannot be removed, so care must be taken not to drop the juice on one's clothes or pocket-handkerchief. Bite the little green pod and you will see a large seed covered with yellow pulp and juice. Suck this and throw away the seeds. The seeds if roasted are somewhat similar to chestnuts.

ENGLISH APPLES AND WOOD STRAWBERRIES

The mountain people bring these into town. They grow in the hills; the apples are not large and the strawberries are wild ones, though at Newcastle and at other high places in the hills the cultivated ones bear and grow to a fair size. The apples are very acid and when stewed take plenty of sugar.

MANGOES

Mangoes are of great variety. Common, Golden, Yam, Beef, East Indian, Number Eleven, Hairy, Black, Kidney, Plummy and so on. The Number Eleven is the best table mango. Some people prefer the commoner sorts and others do not like them at all. The people live on them during the mango season.

NASEBERRIES OR NESEBERRIES

These are very highly appreciated by many people and are called the Jamaica medlar. On the other hand I have heard them called 'mere brown paper and sugar'. They are very sweet. Wash the fruit and eat, skin and all, discarding, if you choose, the seeds and white flaky substance; or eat them with a spoon, leaving aside the skin.

BREADNUTS

The breadnut tree (not breadfruit) has in its pod a large number of nuts, which when roasted are as delicious as chestnuts. They are floury and are served in the same way as chestnuts in a folded napkin at dessert.

CASHEWS

These nuts which grow at the end of the fruit are roasted and eaten with salt and form a pleasing adjunct to dessert. The people make a large fire throwing in the nuts, half of which are over-roasted and spoilt, so that out of four pints you are likely to get two of edible nuts. Do not let your poultry get at them; they give them 'yaws'; a disease of the neck and throat which kills them.

PINDARS

These are ground nuts and can be bought either raw or ready-roasted by the quart. They are very much liked and are eaten with salt. The natives make a sugar cake with the nuts thrown in, as they also do with cashew nuts, and a bean called 'wangla'.

JAMBLANGS

These are a large, long, narrow, very dark, blue-black fruit, not very common but very much liked when they can be had. They are nice in their raw state and excellent as a preserve.

JIMBLINGS

A small blueish black fruit very stainy to the taste but fresh and juicy. They make an excellent preserve.

BIMBLINGS

A sort of berry, very acid indeed. These are generally made into preserve but they take an immense amount of sugar and must be soaked in salt and water before stewing.

CAKES AND BISCUITS

BREAKFAST ROLLS

One pint of flour
One cup of milk
One large dessertspoon of lime-juice
One teaspoon of soda
A little salt

Put the milk into a basin with the soda and salt. Mix it well. Then pour in the lime-juice and whisk all together till it fizzes. Then add the flour and make into small rolls and put them immediately in a hot dutch oven, which must be ready-heated over the fire. Bake. They will take about half an hour.

HOME-MADE BREAD

Very useful in the hills of country parts.

Two pounds of flour
One teaspoon of soda
A little salt
Sour milk

Knead these into a rather stiff dough and bake for one hour.

SCONES

One pound of flour
Two ounces of butter
One large tablespoon of baking powder
A pinch of salt

Mix these ingredients with a little milk. Roll out half an inch thick. Cut into the shapes you please and bake for nearly a quarter of an hour. Then cut in two, butter, cover back. Serve hot.

ORANGE BISCUITS OR LITTLE CAKES, A RECIPE FROM 1809

Whole seville oranges
Equal weight of double-refined sugar

Boil whole seville oranges in two or three waters until most of the bitterness is gone. Cut them and take out the pulp and juice, then beat the outside very fine in a mortar and put to it an equal weight of double-refined sugar beaten and sifted. When extremely well-mixed to a paste, spread it thin on china dishes and set them in the sun or before the fire. When half-dry, cut it into whatever shape you please, turn the other side up and dry that. Keep them in a box with layers of paper. They are for dessert and are also very useful as a stomachic, to carry in the pocket for journeys, for gentlemen when shooting or for gouty subjects.

SNOW CAKE

One pound of arrowroot
Half a pound of pounded white sugar
Half a pound of butter
Four egg whites
Half a teaspoon of essence of vanilla

Beat the sugar and butter till very light indeed and then add the arrowroot, beating briskly. Beat the egg whites to a thick froth and add this, with the essence of vanilla beaten with them, last of all. Beat all well together for nearly half an hour and then put in a pudding pan. Bake at once; it will take about an hour and a quarter to bake; it ought to be very light. Should it colour too soon and seem likely to burn, butter a bit of paper and put on the top while baking.

ARROWROOT CAKES

One pint of flour
One pint of arrowroot
A flat teaspoon of soda
One tablespoon of butter
Sour milk

One pint of flour mixed with one pint of arrowroot and a flat teaspoon of soda. To this add a tablespoon of butter and enough sour milk to make dough. Roll out about an inch thick, cut in squares and bake. To be eaten hot with butter. If you only have fresh milk a squeeze of lime will at once curdle it sufficiently.

CORNMEAL CAKE

One and a half cups of cornmeal
One cup of plain white flour
Two eggs
One tablespoon of butter

One cup of sugar
Enough milk to make it liquid

Rub the butter and sugar together till light. Then add the two well-beaten eggs and dredge in the flour and cornmeal, having first mixed them together well. Add the milk by degrees, just enough to let the mixture pour out thickly. A tablespoon of sherry is a great addition, but it may be omitted. Bake in a buttered tin till it rises well. This will take from half to three-quarters of an hour.

CORNMEAL FRITTERS

One cup of cornmeal
Water
Half a cup of plain white flour
One egg
Lard
Butter

One cup of cornmeal mixed with half a cup of plain flour and enough water to make it liquid. Stir this in a pan over the fire until it thickens. Add a beaten egg and a little butter and fry in fritters with a little lard.

TURNED CORNMEAL

One pint of cornmeal
Water
Spring onions

Tomatoes
Butter
Lard
Salt
Pepper
Salt pork

One pint of cornmeal stirred over the fire with enough water to make it very stiff. Put into it some spring onions, tomatoes, a dessertspoon of butter, a dessertspoon of lard, a little salt, some fresh black pepper and a gill of salt pork cut in dice.

CORNMEAL DUMPLINGS

Cornmeal
Flour
Salt
Pepper

Equal parts of cornmeal and plain white flour well mixed with a little salt, pepper and water into a thick paste; then thrown by spoonfuls, or rolled in balls, into boiling water to harden.

CORNMEAL PAP

Cornmeal
Milk
Sugar

Boil two or three tablespoons of cornmeal to the consistency of pap, then add milk and sugar to taste. Nutmeg over. If you have coconut milk or cream this may be stirred in too. The natives are very fond of this and frequently make their breakfast off it.

STAMP AND GO

Cornmeal
Salt fish
Butter
Flour
Pepper
Lard

These are rough cakes made with cornmeal and flour, rather more cornmeal than flour, a gill of salt fish and a little butter and lard. Pepper, fresh pepper, is freely used. When the mixture is boiled it must be very thick; the salt fish is cut up in small bits before boiling. When cool it is fried in cakes.

The country people as they travel stop at the wayside shops and buy these with slices of bread for a trifle. Hence the name. They are very substantial.

HOMINY CAKES

Hominy
Salt
Lard

Boil some hominy with a little salt. Boil it very thick. Then let it get cool. Cut it in slices or shapes and fry with lard for breakfast.

CORNMEAL DUCKOONOO

Cornmeal
Butter
Sugar
Flour
Spice

A cup of cornmeal boiled thick with some butter, two tablespoons of sugar, a dessertspoon of flour and a little spice. Let it cool. Then roll up in bits of plantain leaf and bake.

HOMINY FOR CAKE, PUDDINGS, BISCUITS OR PAP

It is better to buy this ready-made than to make it at home. The people prepare it from the corngrain by soaking, drying, fanning, sifting, sieving and other tedious processes. It makes excellent pap boiled with milk, or it can be eaten as porridge. It makes a good pudding with the addition of sugar, eggs and spice.

COCONUT CAKES

Three eggs
Ten ounces of sugar
Grated coconut

Three eggs, ten ounces of sugar and as much grated coconut as will form a stiff paste. Whisk the eggs very light. Add the sugar gradually and then the coconut. Roll teaspoons of this in the form of a pyramid; put them separately on paper and bake in rather a cool oven until they are brown.

COCONUT BISCUITS

One pound of grated coconut
Half a pound of sifted lump sugar
Two well-beaten egg whites
Wafer paper

One pound of grated coconut, half a pound of sifted lamp sugar, two well beaten egg whites. Mix these well till smooth, beating the whites first with the sugar and adding the coconut by degrees last of all. Bake on wafer paper in a slow oven.

BREAKFAST CAKES

One cup of flour
Half a teaspoon of soda
Half a teaspoon of salt
A lump of butter the size of a walnut
A lump of lard the size of a walnut
One egg
Bonny or milk

A cup of flour thrown on the pastry board and mixed with a teaspoon of soda and the same of salt. Then add a lump of butter the size of a walnut, and the same of lard. Chop in well. After this beat an egg and mix it with a saucer of bonny or milk: add this to the flour. Mix in to a dough. Roll about a half an inch thick and bake, cut in shapes or sizes to fancy.

BAKED CASSAVA AND BAMMY CAKES

The bitter cassava is grated, pressed and then put into iron hoops or moulds and baked. The bammy cakes are the very thick ones, the cassavas are made in the same way but very little of the thin batter is put at the bottom of the hoops. The cakes are much liked, but it is easier to buy them ready-made, and they are very inexpensive. A packet of cassavas at threepence and a penny-halfpenny worth of bammys are enough for breakfast unless the party is a large one.

CASSAVA CAKES FOR BREAKFAST OR TEA

These little cakes are sold at threepence a packet. There are about eighteen in a packet. They keep for weeks and can be sent to England if liked. Butter them on one side and put them on a gridiron. When half-done, double them over; put them back on the gridiron, and when a light brown and very crisp, send up hot.

Bammys are also sold ready for cooking and are a kind of muffin. These are better eaten fresh, as they do not keep long.

JOHNNY OR JOURNEY CAKES

One pint of flour
One teaspoon of soda
One teaspoon of lard
One teaspoon of butter
A little salt
Water

Mix the flour with the soda. Chop in the lard and butter. Then mix into a dough with enough salt and water to make it easy to roll out. Roll about half an inch thick, cut in rounds with a small tumbler or pan and bake on the gridiron. Open, butter, cover again and serve. I have seen these fried, but they are, in that case, not opened but served intact.

PICKLES

PICKLED LIMES

Limes
Brine strong enough to bear an egg
Fresh water
Vinegar

Half an ounce of cloves
Half an ounce of mace

Make a brine strong enough to bear an egg. Soak the limes for four days, then for a day and a night in fresh water. Boil for an hour, putting them on in cold water. Take them out and put them in a jar or bottle. Boil vinegar with cloves and mace and pour it boiling hot over the limes. When cool, cork them down.

PICKLED PEPPERS

One dozen ripe, one dozen green, also some salmon-coloured if possible, and cherry peppers if they can be had. If you can only get ripe peppers the recipe will apply as well.

Cut as many of them in slices (leaving the cherry pepper whole) as will half-fill a small wide-mouthed bottle. Pour boiling vinegar on them to which a few pimento seeds are added; leave open to cool and then bottle for use.

MANGO PICKLES

Green mangoes
Salt and water
Fresh water
Stuffing of mustard seeds
Dried garlic

Scraped horse-radish or cayenne pepper
Bruised ginger
Allspice
Vinegar
Turmeric
Cloves
Mace
Nutmeg
Pepper
Garlic

Take the mangoes so green as to cut easily; open on the narrow end. Lay them in a vessel of salt and water (strong enough to float an egg) for nine days, or till they turn yellow; exclude the air by close covering to prevent their turning soft. Then take them out of the brine for a few hours. Wipe them quite dry and stuff the inside with the following ingredients: mustard seeds, scraped horse-radish or cayenne pepper, dried garlic, bruised ginger, powdered turmeric, powdered allspice; equal quantities of each for the number you intend to make. Mix all together and fill.

Note. There will be no occasion to tie the mangoes if not cut too open. Boil up as much strong vinegar as will cover them, and to every gallon (or like proportion) put the ounce of powdered turmeric and put on the mangoes. Let them remain for twelve days, then add four pints of vinegar in which you have previously boiled four ounces of cloves, mace, nutmeg and pepper. Beat together. Pour on the whole quite hot and add four ounces of peeled garlic. Tie up the whole very close and in six months' time the pickles will be fit for use. After stuffing the mangoes are put in a jar.

PICKLED MOUNTAIN CABBAGE

Cut as much of the white heart of the mountain cabbage as will nearly fill a wide-mouthed bottle and pour over it boiling vinegar in which you have boiled a few pimento seeds and some whole black peppercorns. Let it stand uncovered until cool. Next day it will be fit for use. A wet cloth is put round the bottle before the boiling vinegar is put in to prevent the bottle from breaking.

SWEET PICKLE OF GREEN TOMATOES

Three pounds of green tomatoes
Salt
Sugar
Vinegar
Cloves
Cinnamon

Three pounds of sliced green tomatoes. Let them stand overnight with a little salt sprinkled over them. One pound of sugar, half a pint of best vinegar, one teaspoon of cloves and two teaspoons of cinnamon. Boil all together for about fifteen minutes, skim and let the syrup boil till thick if preferred, but it is not necessary. Eat with cold meat.

CALABASH PICKLE

Some small calabashes
Salt and water
Slices of pepper
Vinegar
Pimento seeds

Cut each calabash in two; if large cut in four. Very young calabashes are used, the smaller the better. Put them in a basin well covered with strong salt and water for about 24 hours. Slice some peppers. Strain off the salt and water; put the peppers to the calabashes and cover them with good vinegar. This will be fit in about a week. The vinegar must be boiled with some pimento seeds and added boiling and the calabashes must be well drained before the vinegar is added. If the vinegar is not of the best, a growth will form and then pickle will be spoilt.

Savouries and Sauces

Coconut curry

The jelly of a young coconut and its own water
Cinnamon
Curry-powder

Take the jelly of a very young coconut; boil it in its

own water with a little cinnamon, adding curry-powder to taste.

CHO-CHO SEEDS ON SAVOURY TOAST

Remove the seeds without leaving any of the meat or strings around them. Boil these till tender. Put on slices of buttered toast which have a little anchovy spread on them. Pour white sauce over all and serve hot.

CHO-CHO SAVOURY

Two boiled cho-chos
Anchovy toast
Coconut cream

Cut two boiled cho-chos in fingers; put on anchovy toast and pour very hot coconut cream over the whole. Serve hot.

OKRA SEEDS ON TOAST

Take about two handfuls of okra and remove the seeds. Put these seeds on to boil. When half-boiled add a little chopped onion and tomato and season with salt and pepper. Serve when thoroughly boiled, first stirring in a little butter, on buttered toast and send it to table very hot.

WILD CUCUMBER SAVOURY

Butter some toast and spread a very little anchovy on it. Have some boiled wild cucumber ready to place on the toast, and over all pour hot coconut cream.

INDIAN KALE AND POACHED EGGS

Boil the kale till tender and put in a hot dish. Have some poached eggs ready to place on the kale; dust with pepper and serve hot.

BEETROOT

Boil tender. Chop fine and lay in a basin to cool. Turn out and pour a mayonnaise sauce over it.

BEETROOT SAVOURY

Fry a slice of onion in butter; then mix together half a teaspoon of salt, half of dry mustard, half of anchovy sauce, one of flour, three of cream, three of milk. Pour over the onion in the saucepan and fry for five minutes. Lastly, slice in a moderately-sized, ready-boiled beetroot.

If you have no cream, add a little extra milk and flour.

This is to be eaten cold.

CURRIED ACKEES

Twelve ackees
Butter
Rice
Curry-powder

Boil about a dozen ackees; then add a very little butter and some curry-powder. Serve with rice balls. This makes a delicate entrée.

TOMATOES AND EGGS SAVOURY

Tomatoes
Eggs
Butter
Pepper

Boil hard two or three eggs and chop fine. Chop a few ripe tomatoes and add to the eggs; stir together. Put this into a frying pan with a dessertspoon or rather more of butter, some salt and pepper and stir the mixture over the fire for a few minutes. Serve very hot on buttered toast.

SALMAGUNDY

One salt herring
Oil
Vinegar
Tomatoes
Onions
Peppers

Soak a salt herring. Shred with a fork, then pour a sauce of vinegar and oil over it and serve with slices of onion, tomatoes and fresh pepper over it.

CALALOO AND EGGS

One large bunch of calaloo
Four eggs
Butter
Pepper
Milk

There are two kinds of calaloo. The broad-leafed one is used as a table vegetable like spinach. Boil and chop it very fine, then mix with butter and a little milk and black pepper. Add to this some nicely poached eggs put on the top and serve hot.

MOCK DRESSED CRAB

One tin of fresh lobster
Four new-laid eggs
Two tablespoons of cream or good milk
Grated cheese
Essence of shrimps
Mustard
Cayenne pepper
Vinegar
Black pepper
Salt
Breadcrumbs

Drain the liquid from a tin of fresh lobster and divide the flesh into small flakes with two forks. If there is any coral, set it aside for garnish. Boil two new-laid eggs for three minutes (the whites must be like curd). Scoop the whites and yolks from the shell and mix them together in a basin with two tablespoons each of cream or good milk, and the lobster liquid. Add a tablespoon of grated cheese, a tablespoon of essence of shrimps, a dessertspoon of mustard and cayenne pepper, vinegar and salt to taste. Stir the lobster flakes and mix all well together. Fill some crab-shells with the mixture. If you have no crab-shells a small pie-dish will do. Cover with breadcrumbs and put the corals over the garnish. Bake.

SWEET PEPPERS

Three red and three green very large sweet peppers
Mince
Breadcrumbs
Butter

Cut the peppers lengthways and scoop out the strings and seeds. Fill the hollow with highly seasoned fine mince. Cover with breadcrumbs and little dabs of butter. Bake.

SHAD PASTE

Threepence worth of shad fish
Butter
Nutmeg
Black pepper
Cinnamon
Cayenne pepper

Buy threepence worth of shad: it is very salty. Get your cook to scald it and let it cool. The process of making this preparation is tiresome and tedious, but the result is good and it is of great use in the country where fresh meat is not plentiful. Every bone (their name is legion) has to be carefully removed. When you find no more bones, mix in a large tablespoon of butter, half a grated nutmeg, a dessertspoon of black pepper, a teaspoon of powdered cinnamon and a teaspoon of cayenne pepper. Mix all this together well into a smooth paste in a mortar, pounding well, and then put into a jar for use. It is an excellent substitute for anchovy paste with bread and butter, or hot on toast.

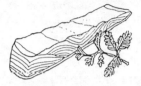

GRILLED SALT FISH

Soak a small piece of salt fish as described on p. 43. Grill it and serve with a roasted green plantain as a savoury.

RED HERRING

Put the herring into a soup plate and pour over it a tablespoon or more of strong Jamaican rum. Set fire to this and when the flame ceases the fish is cooked.

RED HERRING À LA DAUPHINE

Remove the heads, tails and back bone. Soak in warm milk and water. Drain and wipe dry. Dissolve a large slice of butter and mix with the yolks of two eggs and some finely-chopped savoury herbs. Dip the fish into this and spread thickly with fine breadcrumbs. Broil a clear brown over a moderate fire and serve on hot buttered toast sprinkled with a little cayenne pepper.

TOMATO SAUCE

Tomatoes
Cayenne pepper
Shallots
Salt
Vinegar

Sprinkle salt on some very ripe tomatoes; simmer on a slow fire until perfectly soft; strain through a sieve and return them to a saucepan. Season to your taste with cayenne pepper, shallots and salt and allow them to boil until thick; a little vinegar is preferred by many people.

TOMATO SAUCE À LA FRANÇAISE

Six or eight tomatoes
Stock or gravy
A slice of onion
Garlic
A pimento leaf
Vinegar

Take six or eight tomatoes; cut them in two and across. Squeeze out the liquor and put them into some stock or gravy; add a slice of onion, a very small quantity of garlic, a pimento leaf, a sprig of parsley and a spoonful or more of vinegar. Boil together, skim well and serve.

STUFFED TOMATOES

Some large tomatoes
Mince
Breadcrumbs
Butter

Scoop out the centre of some large tomatoes, but not quite all of the pulp. Have ready some well-seasoned mince to press into the hollows. Strew breadcrumbs on the tops with a dab of butter on each. Bake.

PEARS IN CLEAR SOUP

Just before serving clear soup, a small slice of pear peeled and cut into dice can be put in the soup tureen.

TOMATOES AND VINEGAR

Two or three large tomatoes cut in thin slices. Pour cold vinegar over them, and, if liked, add a chopped onion, parsley, oil, pepper and salt: eat with cold meat.

LITTLE EGGS FOR TURTLE SOUP

Beat the yolks of three hard-boiled eggs in a mortar and make into a paste with an uncooked yolk. Roll into small balls and throw them into boiling water for two minutes to harden.

PEPPER WINE

Eight yellow and eight red peppers cut in small pieces, or sliced, and put into a glass bottle or jar. Pour half a pint of sherry on this and put in the sun for twelve hours. It is then fit for use. If you can get cherry peppers, the green and red mixed look very pretty together; some people prefer the tiny bird peppers which are commonly to be had. A little pepper wine is a very great addition to soups or made dishes.

PEPPER VINEGAR

Can be made in the same way as pepper wine; or the vinegar can be boiled and thrown over the peppers whilst hot. It is also used for made dishes and in pea soup.

CHUTNEY SAUCE

Three and a quarter pounds of ripe mangoes
Half a pound of raisins
A quarter of a pound of green ginger
A quarter of a pound of garlic
A quarter of a pound of tamarind

One bottle of vinegar
Half a pound of sugar
Half a pound of salt

Stone, peel and cut the mangoes in bits. Stone and add the raisins. Cut the ginger in dice. Finely chop the garlic. Scrape the tamarind and add the pulp, discarding the seeds. Mix in the salt and the sugar, boil the vinegar and pour it over the whole. Leave open till cold, then bottle for use.

POOR MAN'S SAUCE

Two platefuls of sliced ripe peppers
One plateful of shallots
One ounce of slightly bruised mustard seed
Half a pint of pork or herring pickle

This should be boiled twice over, each time straining and letting it cool. Then boil it up and, while hot, pour it over the ingredients. When cool, add three large onions and a pint of the best white wine vinegar. Cut everything very small. Bottle when cool.

SHADDOCK BITTERS

The people make this by steeping the shaddock-peel with a small bit of orange-peel (both dried) in rum or brandy. This is put in a corked bottle and exposed to the sun for a week.

DRINKS

PIMENTO DRAM NO. 1

Two pints of ripe pimento berries
Two pints of rum
One pint of lime-juice
One gallon of sugar
Four pints of hot water
A quarter of a pound of cinnamon

Put the berries into the rum and lime-juice and allow them to stay there for two days. Make one gallon of sugar and four pints of hot water into syrup; add a quarter of a pound of powdered cinnamon to the hot syrup. When the syrup is cool, add the rum etc. in which the berries have been steeped.

PIMENTO DRAM NO.2

Eight pints of ripe pimento berries
Two bottles of brandy or good old rum
One and a half or two pounds of loaf sugar
A little water

Pour eight pints of ripe pimento berries into a jar and boil till the berries burst. Bruise them well and put them in a gallon bottle. Add two bottles of brandy or good old rum. Let this remain for two months, shaking it frequently. Pass out the juice by squeezing it through a coarse, thick cloth and then add a thick syrup of loaf sugar, say one and a half or two pounds with very little water. If too sweet add another pint of spirit.

PUNCH AFTER TURTLE SOUP

One tablespoon of sour lime-juice
Two tablespoons of sweet sugar
Three tablespoons of strong rum
Four tablespoons of weak water

Mix.

PRUEN LIQUEUR

Half a bushel of pruen seeds
Twelve gallons of proof rum
Four gallons of water
Fifty pounds of good sugar

Half a bushel of pruen seeds just as they commence to germinate thrown into twelve gallons of proof rum: to remain seven days. Strain it: then dilute it with four gallons of water in which fifty pounds of good sugar have previously been dissolved.

Not to be used for two years.

RUM SHRUB

To a gallon of rum, add one and a half pints of lime-juice, three pounds of white sugar and two ounces of crushed bitter almonds.

Bottle for use when made.

FALERNIUM À LA BARBADOS

One gallon of lime-juice
Twenty pounds of sugar
Three gallons of rum
Four gallons of water

Sometimes a few sweet oranges are added. The limes

are to be carefully peeled and squeezed into the rum. Add the ingredients mixed together and put into a cask to clear.

SANGAREE

One and a half wineglasses of sherry
Two wine glasses of water
Nutmeg
Lime-peel
Sugar

Put the water and about a dessertspoon of sugar into a tumbler first. Grate nutmeg upon it: stir. Then put in a long strip of lime-peel. Stir well, adding the sherry last. Mix and serve with a bit of ice in it. This is for one person.

ESSENCE OF GINGER

Three ounces of freshly grated ginger
Two ounces of thinly cut lemon-peel
Two pints of brandy or proof spirit

Put three ounces of freshly grated ginger and two ounces of thinly cut lemon-peel into two pints of brandy or proof spirit (white rum). Let it stand for ten days, shaking it up well.

TAMARIND DRINK

This is very simply made by putting enough of the preserved fruit into a tumbler of water to suit the taste. It is well stirred, strained and taken well iced.

PINEAPPLE DRINK

One pineapple
Three pints of water
One small piece of chewstick-peel
One tiny piece of ginger-root
One pound of sugar

One pineapple, cut in thin slices, the rind as well. Put into a large jar with three pints of cold water, a small bit of chewstick-peel and, if liked, a tiny bit of bruised ginger. Cover and leave till the next day, then strain and mix with one pound of sugar. Bottle this, and either the next day or the day after it will be fit for use. It will effervesce. It does not keep long.

SOURSOP DRINK

One large soursop
Two pints of boiling water
Sugar to taste

Open the soursop and take out the seeds. Put the pith into a large jar or jug. Pour two pints of boiling water on it and strain, after pressing out the juice and stirring well. Then add sugar to taste. Let it cool. A refreshing drink for midday.

PLANTAIN DRINK

Gather the fruit when quite ripe, pull off the skins and mash them in well-boiled water. Let them stay for a night then strain and bottle up the liquor and in a week it will be ready to drink. It is a very pleasant and strong drink, but it should be drunk sparingly as it is stronger than sack and apt to mount to the head.

(This is an old recipe and no mention is made of proportions of plantains to water.)

LIME SQUASH

Limes can be used in every way that the English lemon is. Lemons are sometimes to be procured in the markets and in the country parts, but are not as common as limes. One pleasant preparation is lime squash.

Two limes
Ice
Soda water

Put the juice of two limes into a tumbler. Add some crushed ice, pour a bottle of soda water on this and drink. It is particularly refreshing in the height of summer.

GINGER BEER

Scraped ginger
Water
Chewstick
Lime-juice
Cream of tartar

Scrape some ginger and put it in a mortar. Put a small quantity of water in a large pan (or whatever you arc going to set the beer in). Have the ends of two bits of chewstick beaten and stir in the water till you get a good head, then put in the ginger, a little lime-juice and cream of tartar or soda and add as much water as to make up the quantity of beer you want. Cover up and put in the sun for a day; strain and sweeten to taste and leave till next day. Strain again and bottle and put in the sun for one day more. It is then ready for use.

STRONG GINGER WINE

A twenty gallon cask
Six pounds of ginger
Water
Fifty pounds of sugar
Five gallons of rum

Ten pints of lime-juice
Eggs

Bruise and boil the ginger in water for two hours. (You must have ten gallons of water after boiling.) Dissolve the sugar in this and strain it into the cask; add five gallons of the rum (19° proof) and the lime-juice (half of which has been squeezed with the rind on). Stir every morning for three weeks. Fine it with the whites and shells of four eggs and in three weeks it will be fit to drink.

CURAÇAO

Three-quarters of a pound of dried seville
orange-peel
One and a quarter pounds of shaddock-peel
Eight pints of rum or brandy
Five pounds of sugar
Three pints of water
Lime-peel

Take three-quarters of a pound of dried seville orange-peel and a quarter of a pound of shaddock-peel. Wash well in warm water, changing the water three or four times to extract the bitterness. Dry it a little in a cloth. Put it into a jug with eight pints of rum or brandy. Place the jug or demijohn in the sun daily for a fortnight, shaking it well each time. Dissolve five pounds of sugar in three pints of water; boil it to a thick syrup; strain off the spirit and add to the syrup when cold. When bottling, grate a very little lime-peel into each bottle.

ORANGE WINE NO. 1

Eight pints of sweet orange-juice
Two pints of lime-juice
Five pints of good brown sugar
Five pints of strong rum
Half a pint of milk

Mix together. Put it into a large jug or jar and let it remain three days. Add two tablespoons of temper lime with half a pint of fresh milk. Mix up well. Let it stay for three or four days. Strain and bottle. The lime may be omitted and the whites and shells of two eggs put instead to clear the wine, first taking off the inside skin of the eggs.

ORANGE WINE NO. 2

A twenty gallon cask
Seven gallons of rum
Three gallons of seville orange-juice (oranges with
rinds on)
Three gallons of seville orange (well peeled)
One and three-quarter gallons of sweet orange-juice
(oranges peeled)
Thirty pounds of sugar

Mix together. To be stirred well every ten days.

JAMAICA CHOCOLATE

The cocoa bean is bought by the quart. It is parched and the outer skin pinched off. It is then beaten fine in a mortar and left till quite cool. When hard, it is pounded with spices, sugar and sometimes with a little milk, then rolled into balls and left to harden.

Half a ball makes a cup of good chocolate when grated and mixed very smooth. If not sweet enough, add sugar to taste. This chocolate makes excellent puddings. The balls are sold at a penny-halfpenny each.

NEW SUGAR

Is infinitely preferred by the natives even to 'shop sugar'. It is made in the island at their small settlements and is sold in its unrefined state either as molasses or, firmer, as pan sugar. Mixed with water to which a squeeze of lime-juice has been added, they call it either 'cool drink' or 'beverage'.

HERBAL REMEDIES AND HOUSEHOLD HINTS

MILK

Should the cow's milk be 'weedy' (or tasting of guinea-hen weed to which the cattle are partial), put about a teaspoon of pounded saltpetre in a basin and pour the milk in it; this will remove the disagreeable flavour.

HONEY

Honey is sold at 6d per quart bottle, not by the chemists who sell it much dearer. It is best to buy it from the people who keep bees. The flavour of Jamaican honey is very delicate and it is said that in England, when taken there, it does not harden in winter.

SALT BUTTER

If salt butter is very salty, wash it in water with a squeeze of lime-juice in it; this will remove the salt flavour. If iced it is very good. Some people wash the butter in fresh milk; this is a good plan if you have no limes.

BIRD PEPPERS

Bird peppers make excellent cayenne pepper. They must be put on a tin sheet and exposed to the sun until quite dry and crisp, then pounded in a mortar and sieved through fine muslin.

BANANAS

Bananas eaten with a squeeze of lime-juice are much
appreciated by lovers of this fruit.

SALTED PEANUTS, A SUBSTITUTE FOR
SALTED ALMONDS

Remove the shells and pour boiling water over the
nuts until the red covering leaves them. Spread on a
flat tin, pour salad oil over them and place on a slow
oven for about half an hour. Then sprinkle with very
fine salt, shake thoroughly and set aside to cool.

PUSLEY AND TOONA AS A POULTICE

In cases of inflammation, the poorer people, who
cannot afford a doctor or who are too far away to
send for one, gather these two herbs, boil and chop
them fine and make a poultice which they put over
the inflamed part, adding a little turpentine if the
inflammation is very high.

POMEGRANATE SKIN

Dried, is boiled with arrowroot, red guava root and
logwood for dysentery. It also is used for making
bitters.

WILD PARSLEY

Is used by the washerwomen in the water they wash with to rub the clothes as well as soap. It appears to possess cleansing properties.

TO DESTROY BUGS

One pint of proof rum
Threepence worth of camphor
Threepence worth of calomel
A penny-halfpenny worth of penny-royal

Mix well and put in crevices.

BUSH BATH

Four pints of water
Ackee leaves
Soursop
Joint-wood
Pimento
Cowfoot
Sage
Velvet leaf
Guava
Jack-in-the-bush
Thistle
Cerasse
Elder

Lime leaf
Liquorice bush

This bush bath is firmly believed in by all Jamaicans. In fact it is considered absolutely necessary after fevers or other illnesses. Children in high fevers are lifted out of bed into this bath (first wetting the head with cold water), dried quickly and put back into bed and covered well. Soon afterwards the patient falls into a deep refreshing sleep and the perspiration comes out freely.

Boil up four pints of water with leaves of ackee, soursop, joint-wood, pimento, cowfoot, sage, velvet leaf, guava, jack-in-the-bush, thistle, cerasee, elder, lime, liquorice bush; a few of each or as many of them as you can get. Make the water for the bath as hot as the patient can bear, having thrown the bush tea mixture into it, sponge well, under a sheet thrown over the bath. Dry well, still under the sheet, quickly put on dry clothing and put into bed, covering with bedclothes.

BROOMWEED

Is boiled and used as hairwash; it is very strengthening to the roots.

Wild rosemary

Is boiled and used as hairwash.

Salandine

Is used for cleaning floors.

To destroy blight on plants

Four ounces of bitterwood
Eight pints of cold water
Four ounces of brown soap

Put the bitterwood into the cold water. Boil for ten minutes, then add the grated brown soap and stir in well.

Lignum vitae

The leaves are boiled down to renew black cloth when rusty. The gum of the tree when steeped in rum is good for wounds. Used for the teeth, it will ease pain if the tincture is put on cotton-wool and inserted in the cavity.

FOR A SORE THROAT

Boil a handful of goongoo leaves; add a little new sugar, a teaspoon of vinegar and enough powdered alum to go into an eggspoon. Mix warm, and when cool use as a gargle.

TOONA OR COCHINEAL PLANT

The natives esteem this most highly and use it freely in cases of inflammation or fever. They slice the leaves and lay them on the inflamed part; use it for headaches, fevers, etc; and even boil and drink it when the fever runs high. They also make poultices of it and put it in baths. It possesses very cooling properties.

MARENGA ROOT AS A CURE FOR RHEUMATISM

Marenga root steeped in rum. Tie a flannel wetted with it on the painful part when going to bed. Wipe dry in the morning.

MARENGA OIL

Oil is extracted from the marenga plant. It is considered particularly pure and excellent for delicate machinery such as watches, etc.

CURE FOR DYSENTERY

The natives boil together some red guava root, dog-wood and dry pomegranate skin and mix this with arrowroot made into a thick pap. A spoonful is to be taken every now and then by the patient, the astringent properties being in their eyes as good a cure as 'doctor's physic'.

PEPPER LEAVES

Pepper leaves with a little lard spread over them and applied to a painful boil bring the boil to a head.

CALABASH TEA

For a bad cold attended with cough, one of the native remedies is to boil the leaves of the calabash. Sweeten the tea and take a cupful of it when going to bed and another the first thing the following morning.

GINGER TEA

One small piece of ginger-root
Water
Sugar

Boil a small piece of ginger-root in half a pint of water till it tastes strongly of the ginger. Sweeten to taste. It is taken for spasms or indigestion and can be served with or without a little milk.

CALABASH SYRUP

One full calabash
Some ackee leaves
One sprig of thistle
One or two velvet leaves
Some liquorice bush
One or two cowtail leaves
One or two cowfoot leaves
Some garden balsam
The juice of four or five seville oranges

This is a splendid remedy for colds and coughs. Take a calabash that is full. Scoop out all the inside and throw away the seeds. Put it into a jar without adding any water and put with it a few ackee leaves, a sprig of thistle, one or two velvet leaves, some liquorice bush, one or two cowfoot leaves, one or two cowtail leaves and some garden balsam. Cover and steam for three hours. Then strain and measure how many pints of liquor you have. To each pint, put one pound of brown sugar and let it boil down to a thick syrup. Add the strained juice of four or five seville oranges. Bottle when cool. A small teaspoonful to be taken occasionally.

FEVER GRASS TEA

Fever grass is a fragrant smelling lemony grass; it is excellent in fever just boiled and sweetened or even without sugar. The natives use it freely in fever as it throws one into a profuse perspiration.

VERVINE TEA

The people use the leaves of the vervine plant as a refreshing morning tea sweetened to taste.

BARBADOS RIDE TEA

The leaf of this plant is sometimes used by the people instead of senna.

WILD SAGE TEA

Boil up a few sage leaves and sweeten with brown sugar. If a little wild parsley and thistle is added, it is excellent for colds and coughs.

PIC-NUT TEA

Boil the leaves for a tea; sweeten and serve, hot or cold.

COWFOOT LEAF TEA

The leaves are boiled and used as a drink when one has a troublesome cough.

BITTER BUSH TEA

Boil the leaves as you would tea, and drink for fever or for the liver. It is especially good in diarrhoea. Mixed with old rum, it is taken in doses of a teaspoonful two or three times a day for indigestion. It is a powerful bitter.

THISTLE TEA

This is used boiled as tea for bad colds. For neuralgic pains a decoction is made of a small quantity in proportion of two pints of water boiled to a pint and two tablespoonfuls taken before each meal; while at the same time a poultice is made of the leaves mashed up and applied warm to the part affected.

VELVET LEAF TEA

Boil some leaves with some wild parsley and sage. This is for a cough.

CERASEE OR SORASEE

The leaves of this are boiled as a tea. It is very bitter and by no means agreeable, but it is considered most efficacious for spasms and stomach pains.

TEA FOR A BAD COLD

Garden balsam
Thistle
Sugar

A handful of each of these boiled and sweetened: drink warm at bed time.

HERB TEAS

The Jamaicans believe in herbs for their tea. It is surprising what a number there are that they use, some preferring them to tea or coffee. Jack-in-the-bush, cerasee, mint, elder, okra, vervine, sage, search-my-heart, ackee, lime leaf, ginger, fever grass; there seems no end of them – each appearing to them to possess qualities nourishing, cooling or medicinal.

ROSE-APPLE SEEDS

These are poisonous, but it is said that, thrown loose into a wardrobe drawer, they keep cockroaches away.

CURE FOR RHEUMATISM

Slice, or rather split the leaves of semprevivy: roast them and apply them to the affected part. A very good remedy also is made from the leaves of the prickly pear roasted, trimmed, sliced and applied in a similar way.

LIME-JUICE AND HONEY

Mix very thoroughly the juice of a lime with a wineglass of honey.

Take a teaspoonful of this every now and then to relieve a gritty throat.

TO COLOUR FLOORS DARK

Roast a calabash and throw it into the water the floors are wiped with. It gives a very handsome dark stain.

CURRATO FOR WHITENING DRESSERS, TABLES, ETC.

The leaves of the currato are beaten a little just to soften them. The dresser or table is first rubbed down, then scoured with common red brick and then scrubbed with the currato which makes the dresser most beautifully white like new board.

ANTIDOTES

This is a bean which can be procured at most 'doctor shops' (chemists). It is scraped and put into a bottle with rum. Let it steep, putting it in the sun for a few hours. It is used, after bites or stings of spiders, scorpions, wasps, centipedes, bees, etc., rubbed well into the bitten place.

TO RENEW FADED BLACK CLOTH

Six pints of water
Two pounds of chipped logwood
One and a half ounces of salt of steel
Two ounces of gum arabic
One packet of ink powder
Four outer pomegranate skins

The logwood and pomegranate skins are to be boiled together in six pints of water for four hours. When cool, add the salt of steel, gum arabic and ink powder. The mixture should remain uncovered for one day. After this, strain it through a piece of fine muslin and bottle. The longer it is kept, the better the dye. Cloth to be refreshed should be slightly damped and after it is dry a warm iron passed over it. When perfectly dry to be brushed with a hard brush.

PAWPAW FOR BLACK DRESSES, ETC.

The leaves are used steeped in water in which black dresses, black stockings, etc., are washed in order to retain the black dye.

MEALS FOR A SMALL FAMILY

BREAKFASTS

Monday
Coffee, coconut water
Boiled snappers with butter and parsley sauce
Mashed yam
Salt fish balls
Bammy cakes

Tuesday
Tea, coffee
Curried shrimps and rice
Poached eggs on calaloo or Indian kale
Roasted stuffed white yam
Fried plantain

Wednesday
Tea, prepared kola
Salt fish and ackees
Scaveeched king-fish
Cassava cakes
Roasted cocos
Tomatoes and vinegar

Thursday
Coffee, cocoa
Fried king-fish
Mince balls of kid mutton
Cornmeal toasted in slices
Boiled yam

Friday
Tea, coconut water
Salt fish pie or 'twice-laid'
Roasted breadfruit
Grated yellow yam
Hashed kid mutton with macaroni

Saturday
Chocolate, tea
Oyster or fish omelettes
Cutlets of kid mutton with mushroom sauce and
lime-juice in the gravy
Roast plantain
Yampees

Sunday
Coffee, prepared kola, tea
Curried lobster with rice
Birds on toast
Boiled sweet potatoes
Johnny cakes or breakfast rolls
Cold meat

LUNCHEONS

Monday
Rice and peas
Roast plantain
Lettuce
Shad paste
Bread and butter
Salt fish balls or fritters
Baked bananas
Fruit

Tuesday
Liver or 'haslet' of kid mutton
Salmagundy

Boiled sugar beans
Mashed yams
Potato pone
Fruit

Wednesday
Pig's tongue stewed with red peas
Fish cutlets
Mashed cocos
Pineapple jam with coconut cream
Fruit

Thursday
Pumpkin and rice
Salt fish patties
Fried plantains
Mango fool
Fruit

Friday
Curried oysters on toast
Timbale of kid mutton
Green plantain roasted and chopped fine with butter
Boiled yam
Cho-cho tart

Saturday
Sardine salad
Stuffed pumpkin or pumpkin pie
Roast cocos
Wild cucumbers in white sauce
Coconut blancmange

Sunday
Cold meat
Cold kid mutton pie
Mountain cabbage pickle
Mango chutney
Poor man's sauce
Baked yam
Fried ackees
Angels' food
Guava dolce
Fruit

DINNERS

Monday
Pumpkin soup
Entrée of lobsters or oyster patties
Roast meat
Boiled fowl
Mashed yam
Stuffed aubergines
Cho-cho pudding
Wild cucumbers on toast
Birds
Soursop ice-cream
Fruit

Tuesday
Coconut soup
Entrée of stuffed tomatoes
Leg of kid mutton boiled with white sauce
and onions

Roast guinea-fowl
Roast white yam
Indian kale
Spinach
Boiled ackees
Guava pudding
Black crabs
Banana ice-cream
Fruit

Wednesday
Turtle soup
Entrée of fish timbale
Pork cutlets
Stewed beef
Yam balls
Boiled okra
Pumpkin pudding
Oyster and macaroni pudding
Coconut ice-cream
Fruit

Thursday
White pea soup
Entrée of turtle cutlets
Mince balls
Boiled chicken
Boiled yampies
Fried plantain
Coconut pudding
Okra seeds on toast
Custard ices
Fruit

Friday
Okra soup
Entrée of fish patties
Roast beef
Salt fish stewed with rice balls and mashed
curried yam
Fried aubergines
Orange pudding
Devilled kidneys
Pineapple ices
Fruit

Saturday
Red pea soup
Entrée of baked fish
Roast leg of kid mutton
Boiled corned pork with cabbage
Mashed yam
Cho-cho fritters
Mangoes stewed and served cold with custards or
coconut cream
Oysters on toast
Orange ices
Fruit

Sunday
Ackee soup
Entrée of eggs on Indian kale
Round of beef
Turtle stew
Roast yam
Pumpkin fritters
Shrimps
Black crabs or grenadilla fritters
Strawberry ices
Fruit

PUBLISHER'S NOTE

This book first appeared as *The Jamaica Cookery Book* in Kingston in 1893. Written by Caroline Sullivan, it is thought to be the first published work on the island's cooking. Inevitably, it reflects the tastes and attitudes of another time to questions of food and health. A number of the recipes involve large quantities of cream, others cooking in lard, both of which would be avoided by most cooks today. Some of the recipes in this book – for example those for drinks and ices – call for accurate measures, others are, by contemporary standards, remarkably imprecise. We have left them in their original form instead of producing an edition which belongs in a scientifically managed kitchen rather than that of the large plantation house in which this book was so clearly written. Some recipes call for an ingredient – turtle, an endangered species – the use of which is now illegal. We have chosen to republish these and other recipes unaltered, as they are an essential part of the overall picture of traditional Jamaican cooking painted by Caroline Sullivan, and it seems inappropriate to remove such dishes from this edition even if contemporary readers will not prepare them as printed here. In the same spirit we have retained the author's instructions to 'run the soup through a colander' in order to smooth and thicken it, or to pound ingredients with a pestle and mortar, confident that readers with liquidisers and food-processors can adapt the recipes for use in the modern kitchen. Nor have we changed the author's listing of 'a penny-halfpenny worth of salt pork' or 'some large tomatoes' as ingredients. Caroline Sullivan's social views are clearly those of a bygone age, and they remain in this edition as part of the world-view in an island where slavery had been abolished barely half a century before.

With Britain, the United States and Canada all having substantial, well-established Jamaican and other Caribbean communities, readers in these countries should have few problems in finding shops and market-stalls selling the ingredients called for in this book.

We are most grateful to Vicky Hayward and Cristine MacKie for their advice and assistance in the preparation of this new edition, and also to Valerie Franas and Vita Porter of the National Library of Jamaica.

INDEX

Quacho *see* Cassava

Red herring, 146
  à la dauphine, 146
Red pea soup, 18
Rice
  and pumpkin, 55–6
  and salt fish, 38
Ricey coco, 98
Rose-apples, 115
  preserve, 102–3
Rosemary, wild, 166
Rum shrub, 153

Salmagundy, 143
Salt fish, 37–8
  and ackees, 38
  curried, 41–2
  fried, 40
  fritters, 39
  grilled, 146
  patties, 42–3
  preparation of, 43
  and rice, 38
  shredded, 42
  and susumbers, 42
  twice-laid, 41
Salt herrings, 40
Salt mackerel, 40
  cutlets, 41
Sangaree, 154
Sapadillas, 116
Sauce
  poor man's, 150
  tomato, 147
  tomato à la française,
    147
Scones, 123
Seville orange pudding,
  105–6

Shad paste, 145–6
Shaddock, 111–2
  bitters, 150
Snow cake, 124–5
Soups
  ackee, 21
  coconut, 21
  jonga, 20
  lobster, 19–20
  okra, 17
  pepper pot, 22
  pumpkin, 22–3
  red pea, 18
  sugar bean, 17–8
  turtle, 15–7
  white pea, 18
Soursop
  drink, 155–6
  ice-cream, 108
Stamp and go, 128
Star-apples, 116
  and oranges, 116
Strawberries, wood, 118
Sugar, 160
Sugar bean soup, 17–8
Sweet cups, 115
Sweet potatoes, 62
  pone, 74
Sweetsop, 117

Tamarinds
  drink, 155
  preserved, 101–2
  stewed green, 98
Tapicoa, 66–7
  and coconut pudding,
    101
  pudding, 78
Tarts
  cho-cho, 86